FARMHOUSE COOKBOOK

Old-Time Family Favorites

Susan Beckman

Farmhouse Cookbook © 2016 by Susan Beckman. All Rights Reserved

No portion of this book may be copied, retransmitted, reposted, duplicated, or otherwise used without the express written approval of the author, except by reviewers who may quote brief excerpts in connection with a review. Any unauthorized copying, reproduction, translation, or distribution of any part of this material without permission by the author is prohibited and against the law.

Disclaimer and Terms of Use: No information contained in this book should be considered as error-free recipes. Reliance upon information and content obtained through this book is solely at the reader's own risk. The author assumes no liability or responsibility for damage or injury to the reader, other persons or property arising from any use of any product, information, idea or instruction contained in the content through this book. Reliance upon information contained in this material is solely at the reader's own risk. The author has no financial interest in and receives no compensation from manufacturers of products or websites mentioned.

This book is designed to provide general information regarding the recipes covered. These recipes have been handed down in the family or from friends. There is no intent to duplicate already copyrighted recipes. However, some recipes may contain the same ingredients and instructions as other published recipes. Since these recipes are from family members through the generations, the author has no idea where the recipes might have been originally published, if found somewhere else. The author is not held responsible if this book contains duplicates of already published recipes.

Neither the author nor the publisher assume any responsibility for any errors or omissions in ingredients or instructions, nor do they assume any responsibility for any errors committed on the part of the reader.

sbeckmanauthor@aol.com
ISBN-13: 978-0-9911767-0-0
ISBN-10: 0991176700
Printed in the United States of America

Farmhouse Cookbook

Susan Beckman

DEDICATION

First of all I thank God for blessing me
with the talent and desire of cooking.

I dedicate this book to my mother,

MARIE MILLER CLUM,

whose evening hobby was "reading" recipes
in magazines and recipe books.

She had the courage to always try new recipes.

I thank her for the patience in teaching me to cook.

I wouldn't be the cook I am today
if it were not for my mother.

Proverbs 31

TABLE OF CONTENTS

Appetizers & Snacks	5
Beans	25
Beef	33
Breads & Muffins	49
Beverages	73
Cakes & Cupcakes	83
Candy	103
Casseroles	121
Chicken	141
Cookies	167
Desserts	207
Dips	233
Eggs	245
Frostings	257
Ham	263
Jellies & Jams	273
Main Courses	281
Pasta	309
Pastry	323
Pies	329
Pork	347
Potatoes	361
Preserves	381
Rice	387
Salads	405
Sandwiches	459
Sauces	475
Soups	491
Stews	517
Tomatoes	525

Veggies	531
Miscellaneous	557
DIY	575
Tips	591
10 Foods to Eat Every Day	593
Suggestions for Seasoning	595
Substitutions for Ingredients	598
How Much to Buy	600
Equivalents	601
Weights & Measures	603

ACKNOWLEDGMENTS

Many good cooks in my family have crossed my path through the years.

My mother, Marie Clum, taught me the art of planning and cooking a holiday dinner and ensuring everything was ready at the same time. She also taught me to laugh it off when a new recipe turned out to be a flop and ended up in the garbage!

My paternal grandmother, Ann Bartus Fitzgerald, grew up in the Great Depression and taught me to be frugal with food and how to make homemade noodles. But sorry, Grandma Fitzie, I just couldn't tolerate eating neck bones for a meal!

My maternal grandmother, Norma Culot Miller, was not a good cook, but she did pass on a few of her family recipes that are "keepers!"

My mother-in-law, Nancy Holtzapple Beckman, taught me the art of whipping up casseroles, especially Johnny Marzetti!

My birth mother, Aleda Pollock Coverdale, passed on her own made-up recipes, plus taught me to not store potatoes under the kitchen sink!

I especially want to thank my husband, Greg; children, Amy & Wendy; grandchildren, Brittney, Spencer, Marissa & Alaira; and great-grandson, Alex For being my guinea pigs and not being fearful to at least taste a dish that did not appear appetizing!

Susan Beckman

Foreward

Who doesn't have recipes handed down in their family that everyone loves?

Since my family and in-laws were all fabulous cooks, I possess what seems like tons of good recipes. I have no idea where some of them came from originally.

It was difficult to pick a small amount of favorites because they are all on our list of "keepers." So I tried to pick and choose the quick and easy ones.

There might be some advanced recipes which slipped in between these, but that is only because it is so good, I just couldn't leave it out.

Susan Beckman

APPETIZERS

&

SNACKS

Susan Beckman

SHRIMP CHEESE BALLS

6 ounces cream cheese
1-1/2 teaspoon mustard
1 teaspoon grated onion
1 teaspoon lemon juice
4.5 oz. can shrimp (3/4 cups)
Dash cayenne pepper
Dash salt
Chopped peanuts

Mix & chill.

Form into 1/2" balls.

Roll in chopped nuts.

You wouldn't think nuts would taste good with shrimp, but these are delicious. When my mom made this recipe us kids couldn't get enough of them. She only made them once a year around Christmas or New Year's and I think it's because your hands get messy rolling the balls, but it is well worth it in the end!

Susan Beckman

CRAB SPREAD

Two 8-ounce packages softened cream cheese
1 teaspoon lemon juice
1/2 pound or 2 cans crab meat
1 tablespoon chopped dill

Mix all ingredients.

Spoon into 9" pie plate.

Bake 25-30 minutes at 350° or until hot & bubbly.

Serve immediately.

10-12 servings

This is quick, easy, and great for company.

OLIVE-CHEESE BALLS

2 cups shredded sharp cheese
1/2 cup melted butter
1-1/4 cups flour
36 green olives

Mix cheese & flour; add butter & mix. Mold 1 teaspoon dough around each olive; shape into ball.

Place 2" apart on ungreased cookie sheet. Cover & chill at least 1 hour.

Bake 15-20 minutes at 400°.

Susan Beckman

SURPRISE MEATBALLS

Meatballs, 1 bag frozen or homemade
3/4 cups catsup
1/3 cup grape jelly
1/3 cup water

Mix all ingredients, except meatballs. Add to meatballs and stir.

Heat to boiling; reduce heat, cover & simmer 20 minutes.

Can also put cocktail onions or pineapple in center of meatballs.

I cook these in the crock pot. They are great to take to a potluck.

SEASONED CRACKERS

12-16 ounces oyster crackers
1 package Hidden Valley Ranch dressing
1/4 teaspoon lemon pepper
1/4 teaspoon garlic powder
1 teaspoon dill
1 cup oil

Mix spices, add oil, and pour over crackers and stir.

Bake in 200° oven for 15-20 minutes. Stir occasionally.

Susan Beckman

FRUIT AND NUT MIX

9.5 ounces mixed nuts
1 cup quartered dried apricots
6 ounces smoked almonds
3/4 cup dried cranberries
Pieces of rich dark chocolate

Mix in large bowl. Store in airtight container.

KNOX BLOCKS

4 envelopes Knox gelatin
3 small boxes Jell-O (any flavor)
4 cups boiling water

Mix all and pour into a 9 x 13 dish.

Refrigerate. Cut into small squares.

Susan Beckman

BANG BANG SHRIMP

1/2 cup mayo
3 drops Sriracha
Cornstarch
Lettuce
1/4 cup Thai sweet chili sauce
1 # shrimp
Oil for frying
Chopped green onions

Mix mayo with chili sauce. Add hot sauce to taste.

Dredge shrimp in cornstarch. Deep fat fry until lightly brown. Drain on paper towel, put in bowl and coat with sauce.

Serve in lettuce-lined bowl, top with chopped green onions.

Just as good as in the restaurants.

FRIED DILL PICKLES

1 cup flour
1/8 teaspoon pepper
1 egg
Oil for frying
1/4 teaspoon salt
1/2 cup milk
1-1/2 cup dill pickle slices, thin

Mix flour, salt & pepper. Lightly whip egg in separate bowl. Add milk to egg. Heat 2" oil to 325.

Dip pickle slices into flour, then egg mix, then flour again. Carefully place pickles into hot oil. Do not overcrowd.

Fry until golden brown, about 8 minutes, turning once. Drain on paper towels. Serve warm.

4 servings

SUGARED PECANS

1/3 cup butter
1/2 teaspoon cinnamon
1 # pecan halves
1/4 cup sugar
1/4 teaspoon ginger

Heat butter, sugar & spices until butter melts. Pour over pecans; be sure to coat all nuts.

Bake in shallow pan 30 minutes at 275; stir several times.

Cool & store 4-6 weeks.

CHEESE BALL

2 teaspoon horseradish
Two 8-oz cream cheese
Mayo
1/4 teaspoon Worcestershire
1 pkg. Chipped beef
Paprika & parsley

Mix & chill. Mix paprika & parsley & roll ball in it.

I got this recipe from coworkers, right before I got married in 1973. I've been making it ever since.

GOAT CHEESE STUFFED BASIL LEAVES

4 oz. goat cheese, room temp.
2 teaspoon olive oil
1 teaspoon finely grated lemon zest
Pepper
20 large fresh basil leaves
1/4 cup pine nuts, toasted

In small bowl, stir together cheese, oil & zest. Season to taste with pepper.

Place a spoonful of cheese mixture on each basil leave. Sprinkle with toasted pine nuts and drizzle with oil.

SAUSAGE CUPS

1 # Bob Evans original roll sausage
16 oz. won ton wrappers
1 cup shredded Monterey Jack cheese
1 cup shredded cheddar cheese
1/2 cup ranch dressing

Preheat oven to 350.

Crumble sausage into medium skillet. Cook over medium heat until lightly browned, stirring occasionally. Drain.

Spray mini-muffin tins and insert won ton wrappers to form a small cup. Bake 5 minutes Allow wrappers to cool.

Mix sausage, cheeses & dressing together. Fill wrappers. Bake 10 minutes until bubbly.

Susan Beckman

GRANOLA

4 cup uncooked oatmeal
1/2 cup wheat germ
1 cup coconut
1/4 cup dry milk
1-2 teaspoon cinnamon
1/3 cup oil
1/2 cup honey
1 teaspoon vanilla

ADD:
1/2 cup sesame seeds
1/2 cup nuts, raisins, seeds, etc.

Mix dry ingredients. In saucepan, mix oil, honey & vanilla & warm. Add to dry & stir until all is coated.

Spread in long, low pan, greased, & bake at either: 250 for 1 hour or 300 for 1/2 hour.

Turn with spatula often.

Add dried fruits. Cool & store in airtight container.

I made this for my girls all the time when they were growing up. A lot healthier than store bought.

COWBOY CANDY
(Candied Jalapenos)

3 pounds fresh, firm, jalapeno peppers, washed
2 cups apple cider vinegar
6 cups white granulated sugar
½ teaspoon turmeric
½ teaspoon celery seed
3 teaspoons granulated garlic
1 teaspoon ground cayenne pepper

Remove stems from peppers and slice into uniform 1/8-1/4 inch rounds. Set aside.

In large pot, bring vinegar, sugar, turmeric, celery seed, garlic and cayenne pepper to a boil. Reduce heat and simmer 5 minutes. Add peppers and simmer exactly 4 minutes. Use slotted spoon to transfer the peppers into canning jars to within 1/4" head space. Bring syrup to a full rolling boil. Boil hard for 6 minutes.

Pour boiling syrup into the jars over jalapenos. Insert a cooking chopstick to the bottom of the jar two or three times to release any trapped pockets of air. Adjust level of the syrup if necessary.

If you have leftover syrup, and it is likely that you will, you may can it in half-pint or pint jars, too. It's wonderful brushed on meat on the grill or added to potato salad or - or - or - in short, don't toss it out!

Place jars in a canner, cover with water by 2". Bring the water to a full rolling boil. When it reaches a full rolling boil, set the timer for 10 minutes for half-pints or 15 minutes for pints. When timer goes off, use canning tongs to transfer the jars to a cooling rack.

Leave them to cool, undisturbed, for 24 hours. When fully cooled, wipe them with a clean, damp washcloth then label.

Allow to mellow for at least two weeks, but preferably a month before eating. Or don't. I won't tell!

Serve with cream cheese on cracker and top with a candied jalapeno.

My family loves these so much, I had to make my 14-year-old grandson 12 jars of them for his birthday.

Farmhouse Cookbook

Susan Beckman

BEANS

Susan Beckman

BEANS, BEANS, BEANS

15 oz. pinto beans
16 oz. French green beans
16 oz. baked beans
15 oz. kidney beans
1 medium onion, diced
3/4 cup brown sugar
3 strips bacon, diced
1 green pepper, diced
1 cup chili sauce

Drain all beans. Brown bacon; sauté onion in drippings.

Mix all in 2 qt. casserole dish.

Bake uncovered 1 hour at 350°.

I got this recipe from my mother-in-law. It's been a "keeper" ever since.

Susan Beckman

EASY BAKED BEANS

28 oz. baked beans, drained
1 green pepper, finely chopped
1/2 cup brown sugar
1/8 teaspoon ground cloves
1 onion, finely chopped
1 tomato, finely chopped
1/3 cup Coke

Mix beans, onion, green pepper & tomato in baking dish.

Mix sugar, Coke & cloves until sugar is dissolved. Pour evenly over beans.

Bake covered 30 minutes at 350°.

OLD-FASHIONED BAKED BEANS

2 cup northern beans
5 cup water
2 teaspoon brown sugar
1 teaspoon dry mustard
1/4 cup catsup
1/4 # pork or bacon
1/4 cup molasses
1 small onion, chopped
1-1/2 teaspoon salt

Wash & sort beans. Place in 3-1/2 qt. dish with water, onion, salt & meat.

Cook over low heat 6-8 hours. Drain, saving 1 cup liquid.

Add remaining ingredients. Cook 1 hour over low heat.

Sometimes I like the taste of long-cooking, from-scratch baked beans. This is my go-to recipe for that.

Susan Beckman

BEAN SALAD

1 can yellow wax beans
1 can green beans
1 can kidney beans
1 large onion
1 cup oil
1/2 cup vinegar
1/2 cup water
1 cup sugar

Drain beans. Slice onion over beans.

Mix remaining ingredients and pour over beans.

Let set overnight in fridge.

My mom made this a lot when I was growing up. I've tried some of the canned ones from the grocery store, but this homemade recipe is still the best!

MARINATED GREEN BEANS WITH TOMATOES, OLIVES & FETA

2# fresh green beans, trimmed
2 garlic cloves, minced
1 cup Kalamata olives, sliced
2 teaspoon red wine vinegar
1/4 teaspoon pepper
1-1/2 teaspoon salt, divided
1/4 cup olive oil
2 tomatoes, seeded & chopped
1 teaspoon fresh oregano, finely chopped
Two 4-oz packages feta cheese

Place beans in boiling water seasoned with 1 teaspoon salt; cook 6-8 minutes until crisp tender. Drain. Plunge into ice water. Put in shallow serving dish.

Cook garlic in hot oil over med heat 30 seconds or until fragrant; remove from heat. Stir in olives, tomatoes, vinegar, oregano, pepper & 1/2 teaspoon salt. Pour over beans, tossing to coat. Chill at least 3 hours or overnight. Sprinkle with feta cheese. Garnish with oregano sprigs.

Susan Beckman

BEEF

Susan Beckman

PORCUPINE MEATBALLS

1-1/2 pounds ground beef
1/2 cup water
1/2 cup rice
1 teaspoon salt
1 Tablespoon chopped onion
1/2 teaspoon pepper
1 can tomato soup

Mix, rice, meat, salt & pepper, and onion. Shape into small balls.

Blend soup & water; heat until mixture begins to simmer.

Add meatballs. Cook until tender.

I remember my mom cooking these in her pressure cooker. Then we would put the tomato soup gravy over boiled potatoes. If you don't own a pressure cooker, don't let that stop you. I make mine in a skillet now.

HUNGARIAN CABBAGE ROLLS

8 cabbage leaves
1/4 cup milk
1 pound ground beef
1 egg
1/4 cup chopped onion
3/4 teaspoon salt
1/4 cup uncooked rice
1/4 teaspoon pepper
1 package goulash season mix
1 # tomatoes
8 ounces tomato sauce

Boil cabbage in water until outer leaves come off easily; don't cook too long.

Mix beef, egg, onion, rice, milk, and salt & pepper. Roll in cabbage leaves. Mix seasoning mix, tomatoes, & tomato sauce. Pour over cabbage rolls in casserole dish.

Bake at 350° uncovered for about 30 minutes or until bubbly.

My grandmother, Grandma Fitzie, was Hungarian and taught me at a young age how to make this recipe. But I still can't roll them as tight as she used to.

MISSISSIPPI REDNECK ROAST

4-5 # chuck roast
1 packet gravy mix:
   chicken/brown/au jus
1 packet ranch dressing
1 stick butter
5-10 pepperoncini peppers

Put roast in crock pot.

Sprinkle ranch mix & gravy mix on top. Add butter and place peppers around it on top of the meat.

Cook on low 8-10 hours.

The ingredients don't sound like they would go together, but this is good enough for company. Plus it's fast and easy.

Susan Beckman

BEEF TENDERLOIN

4-5 pound beef tenderloin, trimmed & tied
1 teaspoon kosher salt
2 teaspoon unsalted butter, at room temperature
1 teaspoon coarsely ground black pepper

Preheat oven to 500.

Place beef on a sheet pan & pat the outside dry with paper towel. Spread the butter on with your hands. Sprinkle evenly with salt & pepper. Roast in the oven for exactly 22 minutes for rare & 25 minutes for medium-rare.

Remove beef from oven, cover it tightly with foil, & allow to rest at room temperature 20 minutes Remove strings & slice thickly.

Serve with Gorgonzola Sauce.

Note: Be sure oven is very clean or high temp will cause to smoke.

BEEF BOURG

1/2 # bacon, 1" cubed	2 carrots, sliced thin
1 qt. water	2 onions, sliced thin
4 # beef, 1-1/2" cubes	3 teaspoon flour
1 teaspoon olive oil	1 teaspoon salt
3 - 10-oz. cans beef broth	1/4 teaspoon pepper
2 cloves garlic	4/5 qt. red dry wine
1/2 teaspoon thyme	1 recipe pan-braised onions
1 bay leaf, crumbled	1/2 cup vermouth
2 # small white onions	salt & pepper
1/4 cup butter	
1 # mushrooms, 1/4"	
2 teaspoon butter	

Simmer bacon in water 10 minutes Drain & pat dry; brown in heavy skillet 5 minutes; drain on paper towel. Brown meat in bacon drippings & drain on paper towel. Add oil & stir fry carrots & onions 8-10 minutes Return beef & bacon to kettle; add flour, salt & pepper, and mix. Add wine & spices & simmer 1-1/2 to 2 hours.

Prepare onions & set aside. Saute onions in butter 10 minutes Add vermouth; cover & simmer 15 minutes Add salt & pepper & turn onions to glaze.

Saute mushrooms in butter 8-10 min; set aside. Add mushrooms & onions to beef; cover & simmer 10-15 minutes

Serve with new potatoes, noodles or rice and a salad.

BRISKET with CRANBERRY GRAVY

1 medium onion, sliced
3 # beef brisket, halved
16 oz. can jellied cranberry sauce
1/2 cup cranberry juice concentrate
2 teaspoon cornstarch
1/4 cup water

Place onion in crock pot; top with brisket. Mix sauce & juice; pour over beef.

Cover & cook on low 5-1/2 to 6 hours or until meat is tender.

Remove brisket & keep warm. Strain cooking juices, discarding onion; skim fat. In small saucepan, mix cornstarch & water until smooth; stir in cooking juices. Bring to boil over medium heat, stirring constantly. Cook & stir for 2 minutes or until thickened. Thinly slice brisket across the grain; serve with gravy.

SAUERBRATEN

4 # roast
2 onions, sliced
2 bay leaves
6 whole cloves
12 peppercorns
2 teaspoon salt
1 pint red vinegar
1/2 cup boiling water

Put roast in Ziploc with onions & seasonings. Pour vinegar on top & water. Marinate 3 days or more. Turn twice a day with wooden spoons, NEVER pierce with fork.

Drain meat & brown. Add marinade; cover & simmer 3-4 hours. Serve with gingersnap gravy.

GINGERSNAP GRAVY: Remove meat. Add 2 teaspoon sugar & 8 crumbled gingersnaps & cook 10 minutes Thicken with flour & water paste. Boil 1 minutes Season & serve.

My husband is full-blooded German, so I learned to make this old-time German dish.

Susan Beckman

SWISS STEAK

1/4 cup flour
1/4 teaspoon pepper – 1-1/2 teaspoon salt
3 teaspoon oil
3/4 # steak
2 celery stalks, minced
1 large onion, minced
2 carrots, minced
1 # tomatoes
1-1/2 cup beef broth or water

Mix flour, salt & pepper. Sprinkle 2 teaspoons on steak & pound. Turn & do other side. Brown 5 minutes each side. Remove & set aside.

Saute veggies. Add meat. Spoon veggies on top. Add tomatoes & broth. Cover & simmer 1-1/2 to 2 hours OR bake 2 to 2-1/2 hours at 350.

TEXAS HASH

2 sliced onions
1 small green pepper
1-1/2 teaspoon fat
1/2 # ground beef
1 cup tomatoes
1/4 cup raw rice
1/2 teaspoon chili powder

Saute onions & green pepper; add beef. Stir in remaining ingredients.

Put in greased 1-qt. baking dish. Cover & bake 1 hour at 350. Remove cover for last 15 minutes

Susan Beckman

MARY ANN'S SWEDISH MEATBALLS

1 slice bread, crumbled
2 teaspoon catsup
1/4 teaspoon pepper
1/2 cup chopped onion
1-1/2 # ground beef
2 teaspoon flour
2 cup water
1 egg
1-1/2 teaspoon salt
1/4 teaspoon thyme
1 # bulk sausage
2 teaspoon butter
2 bouillon cubes
2 teaspoon parsley

Beat bread, egg, catsup, salt & pepper, & thyme. Cook onion & sausage until done. Add to beef, then add to egg/bread mixture. Mix well.

Cover & chill 1-2 hours or overnight. Shape into 1" balls. Heat butter. Brown meatballs. Cook until done. Remove.

Pour off all but 2 teaspoon fat. Stir in flour. Add bouillon & water. Bring to boil. Put meatballs in sauce.

BEEF JERKY

1 # chuck or round
1/4 cup Worcestershire
1/4 cup soy
1 teaspoon tomato sauce
1 teaspoon vinegar
1 teaspoon sugar
1/4 teaspoon dried onion
1 teaspoon salt
1/4 teaspoon garlic powder

Trim fat & freeze until firm & solid enough to slice into thin strips. Cut across grain, about 1/8" thick & 1" wide. Put in shallow baking pan. Mix ingredients & pour over meat. Refrigerate overnight or at least 8 hours.

Preheat oven to 140º. Remove meat & put on cake rack over cookie sheet in oven. Dry until strips will splinter on edges – 18-24 hours.

Cool before wrapping lightly with plastic wrap. Will keep in closed container 2-4 weeks.

Since I got this recipe, I started using a dehydrator, which is a super time saver.

Susan Beckman

Farmhouse Cookbook

BREADS & MUFFINS

Susan Beckman

BEER BREAD

3 cups self-rising flour
1/2 cup sugar
1 can room-temperature beer
1/4 cup melted butter

Mix flour & sugar well. Add beer & again mix well. Pour into greased loaf pan.

Cut a slit 1" deep down middle of loaf. Pour melted butter over top.

Bake at 350° for one hour.

The first time I made this recipe, I think it was only because I could have an excuse to use beer.

Susan Beckman

BREAD STICKS

1 can of biscuits
1/4 cup butter
Garlic salt
Caraway, poppy, celery or sesame seeds

Melt butter & pour half into 8 x 8 pan or cookie sheet. Roll unbaked biscuits, twisting to 8". Place in pan. Pour rest of butter over tops. Sprinkle with seeds and salt.

Bake at 450° for 8-10 minutes. Let stand 2 minutes.

I use any kind of can biscuits. I find the crescent or flaky ones are the best. And I've also started using a whole stick of butter. But make sure you let it sit after taking out of the oven so that it absorbs the rest of the butter.

DUMPLINGS

1 cup flour
2 Tablespoons shortening
1-1/2 teaspoons baking powder
1/2 cup milk
1/2 teaspoon salt

Mix dry ingredients; then cut in shortening. Add milk all at once & mix lightly just until dough holds together.

Can add parsley or chives (2 Tablespoons) to dry ingredients.

Drop by tablespoon on top of bubbling soup or stew. Simmer uncovered 10 minutes. Cover and simmer for 10 minutes.

CHEDDAR BISCUITS

Topping:
1/3 cup butter
1/4 teaspoon salt
1/4 teaspoon Old Bay
1/4 teaspoon garlic powder
1/4 teaspoon parsley

Biscuits:
2 cup Bisquick
3/4 cup milk
1/4 cup butter, melted
1/2 cup shredded Cheddar cheese

Heat oven to 425. Stir topping; set aside. Stir biscuit ingredients. to soft dough form. Drop dough by 8 spoonfuls onto ungreased cookie sheet.

Bake 16-18 minutes or until golden brown. Immediately brush hot biscuits with topping. Serve warm.

AMISH CINNAMON BREAD

1 cup butter, softened
2 eggs
4 cup flour
2 cup sugar
2 cup buttermilk
2 teaspoon baking soda

MIX:
2/3 cup sugar & 2 teaspoon cinnamon

Cream butter, sugar & eggs. Add milk, flour & baking soda. Put 1/4 of batter into greased loaf pan).

Sprinkle with little less than 1/2 cinnamon/sugar mix. Top with 1/4 of batter. Swirl with knife.

Bake at 350 for 45-50 minutes or until toothpick comes clean. Cool in pan 20 minutes before removing.

Freezes well.

Makes 2 loaves.

SOURDOUGH BANANA BREAD

1/2 cup butter
1 egg
1 cup sourdough starter
2 cup flour
1 cup sugar
1 teaspoon vanilla
2 bananas, mashed
1 teaspoon salt
1/2 teaspoon baking soda

Cream butter, sugar, egg & vanilla. Mix in sourdough starter & mashed bananas.

In separate bowl mix flour, salt & baking soda. Add flour mix to banana mix & mix just until combined. Do not over mix.

Bake in greased 9 x 5 bread pan for 1 hour at 350 or until toothpick comes clean. Cool completely before slicing.

READY MORNING MUFFINS

2-1/2 cup flour
2-1/2 teaspoon baking soda
1 teaspoon salt
1 cup water
1/2 cup molasses
2 cup buttermilk
1/2 cup butter
3 cup oats
1/2 cup brown sugar
1/4 cup white sugar
2 eggs

Mix flour, soda & salt; set aside. Put oats in separate bowl. Boil water, molasses & butter; pour over oats, stir well & cool. Mix sugars, eggs & milk. Add to oats; stir. Fold in flour mixture. Will keep 3 weeks in fridge. Bake at 375 for 25 minutes Cool 5-7 minutes

Variations: Part or all whole wheat; add 1/3 cup nuts, coconut, raisins, blueberries, chopped dates, chopped or grated apple, well-drained crushed pineapple, bacon bits, ham & cheese; drop as cookie batter on lightly greased cookie sheet. Bake at 375 for 10 minutes

ENGLISH TEA MUFFINS

1/2 cup shortening
3/4 cup sugar
1 egg
2 cup flour
2 teaspoon baking powder
1/4 teaspoon cinnamon
Pinch salt
1 cup milk
2/3 cup raisins
Brown sugar
Pecans

Cream shortening & sugar; mix in egg. Mix dry ingredients.; add to cream mix, alternating with milk. Mix in raisins.

Place in greased tins. Sprinkle with mix of brown sugar, cinnamon & pecans. Bake at 350 for 15-20 minutes.

You can find my recipe for sourdough starter in the DIY section near the back of this book.

MONKEY BREAD

2-1/2 cup sugar
4 (10) cans biscuits
4 teaspoon cinnamon
3/4 cup butter, melted

Lightly grease tube pan. Mix sugar & cinnamon in plastic bag.

Separate biscuits & cut in 4 equal pieces. Coat with butter; add to bag; shake to coat.

Gently press pieces into pan. Bake at 375 for 45-50 minutes

Remove & immediately invert.

PARMESAN-PARSLEY BISCUIT FLATBREAD

16.3-oz. can refrigerated jumbo biscuits
2 teaspoon olive oil
Grated Parmesan cheese

Chopped parsley
Kosher salt
Pepper

Preheat oven to 400. Separate biscuits into individual rounds. Pour oil onto baking sheet. Dip both sides of each biscuit round in oil & arrange on baking sheet. Using fingertips, press each biscuit into a 4" free-form flat circle.

Sprinkle each flattened biscuit with 1 teaspoon Parmesan, 1-1/2 teaspoon parsley, salt & pepper.

Bake for 10-12 minutes or until golden brown. Cut into strips.

ROSEMARY-GARLIC BISCUIT FLATBREAD

16.3-oz. can refrigerated jumbo biscuits
2 teaspoon olive oil
2 teaspoon chopped rosemary
2 garlic cloves, minced
Kosher salt
Pepper

Preheat oven to 400. Separate biscuits into individual rounds. Pour oil onto baking sheet. Dip both sides of each biscuit round in oil & arrange on baking sheet. Using fingertips, press each biscuit into a 4" free-form flat circle.

Sprinkle each flattened biscuit evenly with rosemary & garlic, salt & pepper.

Bake for 10-12 minutes or until golden brown. Cut into strips.

SWISS CHEESE BREAD

1-1/2 cup milk
1 teaspoon salt
2 cup grated swiss (8 oz.)
1/2 cup warm water
Egg with poppy or sesame seeds
2 teaspoon honey
2 teaspoon butter or oil
2 packets yeast
5 cup flour

Scald milk & mix salt, oil & cheese. Cool to lukewarm. Dissolve yeast in water & honey. Add to milk. Stir well. Gradually add flour. Knead 5-8 minutes Place in greased bowl, turning to grease top. Rise until double.

Punch down & divide in half. Roll out to 11 x 15. Cut each in 3 strips. Braid loosely. Pinch ends. Place on greased pan. Cover & rise.

Beat egg with 1 teaspoon cool water & brush on. Sprinkle on seeds. Bake at 350 for 40-45 minutes

CRANBERRY ORANGE BREAD

2 cup flour
1-1/2 teaspoon baking powder
1 teaspoon baking soda
1/2 teaspoon salt
1 egg
1 cup sugar

Orange rind, grated from 1 orange
2 teaspoon melted butter
2 teaspoon hot water
1 cup raw whole cranberries
1 cup coarse walnuts
1/2 cup orange juice

Mix flour, baking powder, soda, salt & sugar; set aside. Mix egg with orange juice, rind, butter & water. Fold flour mixture into egg mixture until blended. DO NOT BEAT.

Gently fold in cranberries & walnuts. Spoon into greased 9 x 6 pan or smaller pans of choice.

Bake at 325 for 60 minutes Cool on rack 15 minutes.

Great to make around Thanksgiving or Christmas.

Susan Beckman

NO-EXCUSE BREAD

2 packets yeast
2 teaspoon salt
1/3 cup oil or butter
1/3 cup honey or sugar
7 cup flour
2/3 cup dry milk
2 eggs
1 cup wheat germ (optional)
2 cup warm water

Have all ingredients. At room temp. Put all except flour in large bowl. Add 3 cup flour. Beat 5-10 minutes at medium speed. By hand, stir in 2 cup flour. Sprinkle 1 cup flour in 10" circle. Oil hands & knead in flour 5-10 minutes

Cover with plastic wrap & folded towel. Rest 20 minutes Punch & divide in half. Roll out to 8x12" Roll up. Put seam side down in oiled pan. Cover with plastic. Refrigerate 2-24 hours.

Puncture air bubbles with oiled toothpick. Bake at 375 for 30-35 minutes.

I got this recipe from the La Leche group I belonged to back in the 1970s in Marquette, Michigan. I love it since you don't have to knead it.

DARK DATE NUT BREAD

1/2 cup boiling water
1/2 cup mixed light & dark raisins
1/2 cup chopped dates
1-1/2 teaspoon butter
3/4 teaspoon soda
3/4 cup + 2 teaspoon flour
1/2 cup sugar
1/4 teaspoon salt
1 egg
1/2 teaspoon vanilla
1/4 cup nuts

Pour boiling water over raisins, dates, butter & soda; let stand. Mix flour, sugar & salt, add fruit & remaining ingredients. Beat well.

Pour in greased & floured 1 # coffee can.

Bake at 350 for 60-70 minutes.

I haven't made this in a while because my husband doesn't drink much coffee anymore and I can't ever remember to save the can - or I should say, buy coffee in the can since most are sold in bags now.

NO-KNEAD WHOLE WHEAT FRIDGE ROLLS

2 packets yeast
2 cup warm water
2 teaspoon honey
2-1/4 cup flour
2 teaspoon salt
1/4 cup oil
2 cup whole wheat flour

Dissolve yeast in water; add honey. Sit 10 minutes Add salt & oil. Add whole wheat. Beat with electric mixer 2 minutes Add flour. Mix well. Cover with damp cloth. Can refrigerate several days. Punch down as needed.

When ready to bake, punch down. Pinch off pieces; form into balls & place close in greased pan. Cover & let rise in warm place until almost double – 30-45 mins.

Bake at 400 for 15 minutes or until lightly browned on bottom.

Great to have on hand in the fridge for a quick little homemade rolls.

APPLE CIDER BISCUITS

2 cup flour
4 teaspoon baking powder
2 teaspoon sugar
1/2 teaspoon salt
1/3 cup butter, in chunks
3/4 cup cider
1/8 teaspoon cinnamon

Mix flour, baking powder, sugar & salt. Blend in butter until coarse crumbs. Stir in cider, just until soft dough forms & leaves side of bowl. Turn on floured board. Roll or pat to 1/2"; cut 2" circles.

Place 1" apart on ungreased sheet. Sprinkle with cinnamon & pierce tops with fork.

Bake at 450 for 12-15 minutes.

BAKING POWDER BISCUITS

2 cup flour
3 teaspoon baking powder
1 teaspoon salt
1/3 cup Crisco
3/4 cup milk

Mix flour, baking powder & salt. Cut in Crisco. Add milk; stir with fork until blended. Transfer to floured surface. Knead gently – 8-10 times.

Roll dough 1/2" thick. Cut & bake on ungreased baking sheet at 425 for 12-15 minutes.

GOOD-MORNING MUFFINS

1 cup sugar
1/2 cup butter
1 cup milk
1 egg
1 teaspoon nutmeg
1-1/2 cup flour
1/8 teaspoon salt
2 teaspoon baking powder
1/2 teaspoon cinnamon
3/4 cup wheat germ
3 teaspoon molasses
Dates, raisins, nuts, apricots

Mix in order given. Do not stir too much. Bake in greased or lined muffin pans @ 425 for 20-25 minutes

VARIATIONS:

Apple Muffins: Omit nutmeg, wheat germ & molasses. Add 1 teaspoon grated lemon & 1 cup grated apples. Mix lightly & quickly.

Topping: 1/3 cup chopped nuts   1/3 cup brown sugar   1/2 teaspoon cinnamon

Blueberry or Raspberry: Omit nutmeg, cinnamon & molasses. Add 1 cup fresh fruit.

I should have called these Mary Jo's Good Morning Muffins - she knows why!

Susan Beckman

RYE BREAD
(makes 4 loaves)

3 cups lukewarm water
1-1/2 teaspoon yeast
1-1/2 teaspoon caraway seeds
1 cup rye flour
5-1/2 cups flour
cornmeal & cornstarch

Mix yeast, salt & caraway with water; mix in dry ingredients without kneading. Cover with towel & rest for about 2 hours. Then prepare for cooking or store in fridge for 2 weeks.

Dust surface of dough with flour & cut off ¼ of dough; dust with flour and quickly shape into ball, elongate ball into oval shape; rest & rise on cornmeal surface for 40 minutes. Preheat oven 450, with empty pan on bottom rack.

Mix 1/2 teaspoon cornstarch with water to form paste; add 1/2 cup water, whisk & microwave 1 minute. Paint top of bread with cornstarch & sprinkle with caraway; slash with deep parallel cuts across top of loaf.

Bake for 30 minutes on sheet or baking stone. Put 1 cup hot tap water in pan below & quickly close oven door.

Farmhouse Cookbook

Susan Beckman

Farmhouse Cookbook

BEVERAGES

Susan Beckman

SOUTHERN SWEET TEA

3 cups boiling water
4 cups cold water
1 family-size tea bag or 3 regular
1 cup simple syrup

Pour water over tea bags. Steep 5 minutes. Remove tea bags.

Add simple syrup & water.

Serve over ice.

Makes 1/2 gallon.

Turns out perfect every time.

Susan Beckman

RUSSIAN TEA

2 cups Tang
1/2 cup instant **tea**
1/2 cup lemonade mix
1 teaspoon cloves
1/2 teaspoon cinnamon
1/2 cup sugar

Mix & store. Use a teaspoon or two in cup of hot water.

Got this recipe from my Yooper friend, Sandi Longhini, way back when we were in the Air Force in Marquette, Michigan. My girls insist I make this every Christmas.

KAHLUA

1-1/2 cups water
1 fifth vodka
3-3/4 cups sugar
2 tablespoons glycerin
7 tablespoons instant coffee
2 teaspoons vanilla mixed with 1/2 cup hot water

Boil 1-1/2 cups water & sugar 2 to 3 minutes. Add vanilla. Add coffee mixture.

Pour into half-gallon jug or bottle. Add vodka & glycerin. Stir gently.

Cap & let stand at least 4 days before using.

I never knew you could make your own Kahlua - or at least I never thought about it until I was going through my grandmother's old recipes and found this one. Way to go, Grandma Fitzie!

Susan Beckman

ORANGE BRUTUS

6 cup orange juice
1 envelope Dream Whip
3 oz. vanilla pudding (not instant)

Put 3 cups orange juice in blender with Dream whip & pudding.

Blend on high speed until smooth.

Pour into large pitch & stir in 3 more cups orange juice.

Serve on crushed ice.

HOT COCOA MIX

2 cup dry milk
3/4 cup sugar
1/2 cup cocoa
1 teaspoon salt
1 cup mini marshmallows

Mix & store for 2 months.

Put 2-3 teaspoon in mug & fill with boiling water.

For extra rich, use hot milk.

Susan Beckman

RED ZINGER TEA

Bring 1 gallon water almost to a boil. Add 8 bags Red Zinger herb tea.

Cover & let steep 2 hours.

Mix 64 oz. lemonade with tea & chill.

BRANDY SLUSH

12 oz. lemonade
12 oz. orange juice
9 cans water
1 cup sugar

Mix well & add fifth of brandy.

Put lid on & freeze 24 hours.

Scoop out with ice cream scoop.

Can pour 7-Up over.

My neighbor served this around Christmastime and I begged for the recipe. But I have since learned, don't drink this while making Christmas dinner! I've learned from experience.....

Susan Beckman

CAKES & CUPCAKES

Susan Beckman

BLACK-BOTTOM CUPCAKES

Mix:
8 ounces cream cheese
1 egg
1/3 cup sugar
6 oz. chocolate chips

Beat well & stir in chips; set aside.

Mix:
1-1/2 cups flour
1 cup sugar
1/4 cup cocoa
1 teaspoon baking soda

Add:
1 cup water
1/3 cup oil
1 Tablespoon vinegar
1 teaspoon vanilla

Fill muffin tins 1/3 full with chocolate batter. Top each with heaping spoonful of cheese mixture.

Bake at 350° for 25-30 minutes.

Susan Beckman

RED VELVET CAKE

1/2 cup Crisco
1-1/2 cups sugar
2 eggs
sifted
1 ounce red food color
2 bottles water

Mix by hand:
3 Tablespoons cocoa
2-1/4 cups cake flour

Pinch salt
Then add:
1 cup buttermilk
1 teaspoon vanilla
1 teaspoon vinegar
1 teaspoon baking

soda

Cream Crisco with sugar. Add eggs, water, red food color & cocoa. Then add flour. Then add remaining mixture.

Bake at 350° for 35-40 minutes in two cake pans.

This is another of Grandma Fitzie's recipes she would make every Christmas.

NANCY'S LOAF CAKE

1 box lemon cake mix
1 small box lemon Jell-O
4 eggs
3/4 cup oil
3/4 cup water
1 teaspoon salt

Mix all ingredients for 4 minutes on medium speed. Bake in 9 x 13 dish for 35-40 minutes.

Mix: 2 cups powdered sugar
1/2 cup lemon & orange juice, mixed

While still warm, poke holes in top & drizzle over top.

My mother-in-law gave me this recipe. It is light and refreshing.

BUTTER BRICKLE DESSERT

20 oz. crushed pineapple
1 box butter pecan cake mix
1 stick butter, sliced
1/4 cup brown sugar
1 package butter brickle
Chopped nuts

Grease 9 x 13 dish. Pour pineapple, including juice, in bottom of pan. Sprinkle brown sugar over pineapple.

Sprinkle cake mix over pineapple, then sprinkle butter brickle over cake mix. Put butter slices evenly over top. Add nuts on top.

Bake at 350° for 1 hour. Serve with cool whip.

PUMPKIN PIE CAKE

1 box yellow cake mix (save 1 c)
To remainder ADD:
1 stick melted butter
1 beaten egg

Mix. Press into greased 13 x 9 dish

Mix filling & pour over cake dough.

FILLING:
3 eggs
1#-13oz solid pumpkin
1/2 cup brown sugar
1/4 cup sugar
2/3 cup milk
1/2 teaspoon cinnamon

Using reserved 1 cup cake mix, plus 1/2 cup sugar and 1/2 stick cold butter, crumble together & then add 1/2 cup nuts; sprinkle over pumpkin.

Bake 55 minutes at 350.   Will be jiggly when taken out, but will set up as it cools.

FUDGE BROWNIE RING CAKE

1 pkg. (family size) brownie fudge mix
1 pkg. Coco-Almond or Coco-Pecan frosting mix
1 cup sour cream
2/3 cup milk
2 eggs

Preheat oven to 350 (325 for colored fluted pan). Generously grease & flour 10" fluted or tube pan.

In large bowl, mix all ingredients. Stir well with wooden spoon (not electric mixer). Pour batter in pan. Bake 55-60 minutes Cool 15 minutes, then remove.

Frost or serve with whipped cream or ice cream.

PINEAPPLE UPSIDE-DOWN CAKE

1/2 cup butter
3 eggs
1/4 teaspoon salt
1 teaspoon vanilla
1-1/2 teaspoon baking powder
2 cup brown sugar
1 cup sugar
1/3 cup pineapple juice
1-1/4 cup flour
Pineapple slices

Melt butter in skillet; add brown sugar & pineapple. Can put maraschino cherries in center & nuts.

Separate eggs. Beat yolks until light & smooth. Add sugar, juice & vanilla. Mix flour, baking powder & salt. Stir into egg mixture.

Beat whites until hold peaks. Fold gently into first mixture. Pour over fruit.

Bake 35-45 minutes at 350-375. Start at 375; then when it starts to turn brown, turn to 350.

My mom's favored recipe that she always cooked in a cast-iron skillet that belonged to my Grandma Miller. And I now own that cast-iron skillet!

… Susan Beckman

TEXAS CHOCOLATE SHEET CAKE

2 cup flour
2 cup sugar
1 cup butter
1/2 cup sour milk
1 teaspoon vanilla
3-1/2 teaspoon cocoa
1 cup water
2 eggs
1 teaspoon baking soda

Mix flour & sugar; set aside. Melt butter, cocoa & water. Add to flour & sugar. Beat eggs, milk, soda & vanilla. Mix well.

Bake in jelly roll pan @ 375 for 20 minutes

ICING:

1 box powdered sugar
1 stick melted butter
3-1/2 teaspoon cocoa
1 teaspoon vanilla
6 teaspoon milk
1 cup nuts
Ice while hot.

This makes a lot, so better make sure you're having a lot of people who can eat it up!

TURTLE CAKE

1 package chocolate cake mix with pudding
1 cup chocolate chips
1/2 cup evaporated milk
14 oz. bag caramels
1 cup chopped nuts

Mix cake as directed. Bake 1/2 batter @ 350 for 20 minutes in 9x13 pan.

Melt remaining ingredients & spread on top. Spread remaining batter on top & bake 25 minutes longer.

RICH!!!!

Susan Beckman

PISTACHIO CAKE

1 pkg. Yellow or white cake mix
1 pkg. Pistachio pudding mix
3 eggs
1 cup oil
1 cup chopped nuts
1 cup 7-Up

ICING:

1 pkg. Pistachio pudding mix
1-1/4 cup cold milk

Add:
1 large Cool Whip
1/2 teaspoon vanilla
1-1/2 cup coconut

Bake @ 325-350 in 9x13 pan for 30-40 minutes

COCOA-ALMOND CAKE

1 cup heavy whipping cream
1/3 cup hot cocoa mix
3/4 teaspoon almond
Angel food cake

Beat cream, cocoa & almond flavoring until stiff peaks form.

Spread over top & side of cake. Refrigerate until ready to serve.

10 servings

Susan Beckman

CARROT CAKE

Mix:
4 eggs
2 cup sugar

Add:
1-1/2 cup oil
1 teaspoon salt
2 teaspoon cinnamon
13 oz. crushed pineapple, undrained

ICING:

8 oz cream cheese
1 # powdered sugar
1/2 cup butter
2 teaspoon vanilla

Bake @ 350 for 45-50 minutes

Optional: Orange food coloring for icing

CHOCOLATE VELVET CHEESECAKE

1-1/2 cup graham crackers
1/3 cup melted butter
1/4 cup sugar

Press into 9" spring-form pan.

Bake @ 325 for 10 minutes

16 oz. cream cheese
2 teaspoon vanilla
1/2 cup sugar

Stir in: 4 beaten egg whites

Add: 12 oz. melted chocolate chips

Beat egg whites until soft peaks form. Gradually add 1/2 cup sugar. Fold by hand into cheese mixture. Also add 2 pkgs. Dream Whip & 1 cup finely chopped pecans.

Pour into shell & refrigerate or freeze.

20 servings

My mom made this almost every Christmas or New Year's. It is great for company.

Susan Beckman

COCA-COLA CAKE

2 cup flour
1 cup sugar
2 sticks butter
3 teaspoon cocoa
1 cup Coke
1/2 cup buttermilk
2 eggs, beaten
1 teaspoon baking soda
1 teaspoon vanilla
1-1/2 cup small marshmallows

Mix flour & sugar. Heat butter, cocoa & Coke until boiling. Pour over flour mix & mix. Add butter, milk, eggs, soda, vanilla & marshmallows; mix well. Batter will be thin & marshmallows will come to top.

Bake in sheet pan (12x24x2) @ 350 for 30-35 minutes

ICING:
1 stick butter
3 teaspoon cocoa
6-7 teaspoon Coke

Pour over:

1 box powdered sugar
1 cup toasted chopped pecans

Pour over cake while still warm

HOT FUDGE PUDDING CAKE

1-1/4 cup sugar (divided)
1 cup flour
7 teaspoon cocoa (divided)
2 teaspoon baking powder
1/4 teaspoon salt
1/2 cup milk
1/3 cup melted butter
1-1/2 teaspoon vanilla
1/2 cup brown sugar
1-1/4 cup hot water

Heat oven to 350. In med. bowl mix 3/4 cup sugar, flour, 3 teaspoon cocoa, baking powder & salt. Blend in milk, butter & vanilla; beat until smooth. Pour into square pan (8 x 8 x 2 or 9 x 9 x 2).

In small bowl, mix remaining 1/2 cup sugar, brown sugar & 4 teaspoon cocoa; sprinkle over batter. Pour hot water over top; DO NOT STIR.

Bake 40 minutes or until center is almost set. Let stand 15 minutes Serve with whipped cream.

Susan Beckman

APPLE CAKE

1 cup oil
3 eggs
1-3/4 cup sugar
2 cup flour
1 teaspoon cinnamon
7-8 apples, peeled & sliced
1/2 cup chopped nuts
1/2 cup raisin
1 teaspoon baking soda
Additional cinnamon, powdered sugar & nuts.

Mix oil, eggs, sugar & vanilla. Blend in dry ingredients; mix well. Add remaining ingredients.

Spread in greased 9x13 pan. Bake @ 350 for 1 hour.

Farmhouse Cookbook

Susan Beckman

CANDY

Susan Beckman

SALTED CARAMEL PRETZEL BARK

2 sticks butter
1 regular bag pretzels
Sea salt - coarse
1 cup light brown sugar
12-oz. chocolate chips

Line large pan with parchment, cover with pretzels. In med. pan melt butter over medium-low heat. When begins to bubble, add sugar. Stir occasionally. Let meld together and brown; about 3 minutes. Do NOT let it boil.

Pour over pretzels, slowly & evenly. Spread with spatula; work quickly.

Bake at 400 for 5 minutes. Remove & sprinkle chocolate chips over. Bake 45 seconds. Remove. Use spatula to spread chocolate. Sprinkle with salt. Refrigerate for minimum of 1 hour.

Susan Beckman

DADDY'S FUDGE

3 cups semi-sweet chocolate chips
2 Tablespoons butter
1 can Eagle Brand milk
1 cup walnuts
1/2 jar peanut butter
1 small bag marshmallows (a portion)
1-1/2 teaspoon vanilla

Melt chocolate chips, butter, milk & peanut butter in microwave for 4 minutes at 50%. Remove & mix well.

Add vanilla & nuts, mix; add a portion of the bag of marshmallows & mix.

Pour in 8 x 8 pan, then refrigerate until hard.

My dad never cooked much but he found this was one recipe he never failed at. When we went to their house he was always so proud when he made his fudge that you didn't dare refuse to try it!

ELAINE'S FUDGE

4 cup sugar
13-16 oz. marshmallow cream
16 oz. chocolate chips
1-1/3 cup milk
16 oz. chunky peanut butter
2 teaspoon vanilla

Butter sides of heavy saucepan. Mix sugar & milk. Heat & stir over medium heat until begins to boil. Cook to soft-ball stage.

Remove from heat & add remaining ingredients. & stir until blended. Pour into buttered pan; score in squares & let cool.

PEPPERMINT BARK

White chocolate
Peppermint candy canes, crushed

Melt white chocolate. Spread in parchment-lined or foil-lined baking sheet. Sprinkle crushed peppermint on top & press lightly.

Let cool. Break into random pieces

SALTY CHOCOLATE-PECAN CANDY

1 cup pecans, coarsely chopped
3 (4-oz.) bars bittersweet chocolate baking bars
3 (4 oz.) white chocolate baking bars
1 teaspoon coarse sea salt or kosher salt

Place pecans in single layer on baking sheet. Bake at 350° for 8-10 minutes or until toasted. Line 12 x 17 jelly roll pan with parchment paper. Break each chocolate bar into 8 equal pieces. Arrange in checkerboard pattern in pan, alternating white & dark chocolate. Pieces will touch.

Bake at 225° for 5 minutes or just until chocolate is melted. Remove pan to wire rack. Swirl chocolate into marble pattern using wooden pick. Sprinkle evenly with toasted pecans & salt. Chill 1 hour or until firm. Break into pieces. Store in airtight container in fridge up to 1 month.

Susan Beckman

TOOTSIE ROLLS

12 oz. semisweet chocolate chips
3/4 teaspoon warm water
1/2 cup light corn syrup
1-2/3 teaspoon orange flavoring

Line baking tray with plastic wrap; set aside. Melt chocolate in microwave. Stop to stir every 5-10 seconds. Add remaining ingredients. & stir well. Scrape mixture onto tray & press down with back of spatula to 1" thickness. Will not cover pan. Cover with plastic wrap. Sit overnight at room temp.

Peel off wrap & cut into 1/2"-3/4" wide strips. Form each strip into log & roll until 1/2" in diameter. Cut into sections; set aside few minutes to harden. Wrap in waxed paper or colored foil squares.

This is something I've found fun to sometimes make with my grandkids when they come to sleep over.

MIXED NUT BARS

1-1/2 cups flour
1/2 cup + 2 Tablespoons butter, divided
3/4 cup brown sugar
1 can (11-1/2 oz.) mixed nuts
1/4 teaspoon salt
1 cup butterscotch chips
1/2 cup light corn syrup

In bowl, combine flour, sugar & salt. Cut in 1/2 cup butter until mixture resembles coarse crumbs. Press into greased 9 x 13 x 2" baking pan. Bake at 350° for 10 minutes.

Sprinkle with nuts. Melt butterscotch chips. Add corn syrup & remaining butter; mix well. Pour over nuts. Bake 10 minutes.

Cool. Cut into bars.

CRACKER JACKS

1/2 cup honey
1/4 cup butter
6 cups popped corn
1 cup peanuts

Heat honey & butter. Cool. Pour over popcorn which has been mixed with peanuts.

Spread in pan & bake at 350° for 5-10 minutes or until crisp.

BUCKEYES

1 box (16 oz.) powdered sugar
1 teaspoon vanilla
1-1/2 cups peanut butter
1/2 teaspoon salt
1/2 cup soft butter

Mix together and shape into balls.

Melt together:
12 oz. chocolate chips
1 square paraffin wax

Dip balls into chocolate mixture with toothpicks & cool on wax paper.

If you don't know what buckeyes are, you won't appreciate these. Ohio is known for their buckeye trees and this candy looks almost like the real thing. But at least you can eat these!

Susan Beckman

CARAMELS

1 cup butter
Dash salt
15 oz. condensed milk
1 teaspoon vanilla
1 # brown sugar
1 cup corn syrup

Melt butter in 3 qt. pan. Add sugar & salt. Blend in syrup. Gradually add milk; stirring constantly.

Cover over medium heat until reaches firm-ball stage (245) – 12-15 minutes

Remove from heat; stir in vanilla. Pour in buttered 9x9 pan. Cool.

My mom made these every year about a week or two before Christmas. We were lucky if there were any left by the time Christmas came along.

NO-COOK DIVINITY

1 box fluffy white frosting
1/2 cup boiling water
1/3 cup corn syrup
1 teaspoon vanilla

Beat on highest speed in large bowl until stiff peaks form – 5 minutes

Blend in:
1 # powdered sugar gradually
1 cup nuts, stir in

Can add food coloring & flavorings. Drop onto waxed paper. Wen outside feels firm, turn over. Allow to dry 12 hours or overnight.

Susan Beckman

CARAMEL CORN

1/2 cup butter
1/4 cup corn syrup
1/4 teaspoon baking soda
1 cup brown sugar

1/2 teaspoon vanilla
1/2 teaspoon salt
3 qt. popped corn (1/2 cup unpopped)

Melt butter; stir in sugar, corn syrup & salt. Bring to boil; stirring. Boil over med. heat 5 min; NO stirring. Remove from heat; stir in baking soda & vanilla. Pour over corn, mixing well, on buttered, foil-lined flat pan, mix.

Bake uncovered @ 300 for 10 min; stir; bake 10 minutes WATCH. Remove & cool. Break into pieces. Store in tightly covered container.

TAFFY

1-1/4 cup light molasses
3/4 cup sugar
1 teaspoon vinegar
1 teaspoon butter
1/8 teaspoon soda
1/8 teaspoon salt

Blend molasses, sugar & vinegar. Place over low heat & stir until mixture boils. Cook to 270º, stirring occasionally. Remove pan from heat & add butter, soda & salt. Pour on a buttered platter.

When cool enough to touch, oil hands lightly with butter & pull until taffy is a light golden color. Cut candy into pieces & wrap in waxed paper.

Makes about 1 pound.

Susan Beckman

RUM BALLS

2 cup crushed vanilla wafers
1 cup chopped nuts
1 cup powdered sugar
2 teaspoon cocoa
1/3 cup rum
2 teaspoon corn syrup

Mix & roll into balls (walnut size). Roll in powdered sugar.

Makes *20 balls.*

These are my sister's favorite. She took some to high school one day and was eating them in study hall. The teacher came along and wanted to know what she was eating. She gave him one and all he could do was raise his eyebrows and smile!

Farmhouse Cookbook

Susan Beckman

CASSEROLES

Susan Beckman

TURKEY CASSEROLE

2 – 10-oz. frozen broccoli, cooked
2 cup cooked cubed turkey
1 teaspoon onion
1/4 cup oil
1/4 cup flour
2 cup milk or chicken stock
1 teaspoon salt – 1 cup mayo
1 teaspoon lemon juice
1/2 cup bread crumbs
1/2 cup cheese

Put broccoli in greased casserole dish. Cover with turkey.

In pan mix oil, flour, milk or stock over med. heat. Stir constantly until boils. Add salt, onion, mayo & lemon juice. Pour over turkey. Top with crumbs & dot with butter. Sprinkle cheese on top.

Bake uncovered @ 325 for 25 minutes

Susan Beckman

SAUSAGE & CHEESE GRITS

2# sausage, browned & drained
1-1/4 cup quick cooking white grits
1 cup milk
1/8 teaspoon garlic powder
paprika for garnish
4 cup water
4 cup (1#) shredded sharp cheese
½ teaspoon thyme
4 eggs, lightly beaten

Boil water & stir in grits. Cover & reduce heat to low simmer for 5 minutes. Stir frequently. Remove from heat & stir in cheese, milk & seasonings. Add sausage & eggs.

Pour into 13x9 dish. Bake at 350 for 1 hour or until golden brown.

Can be prepared the night before & baked the next day.

I hate grits, but I like this recipe. It makes quite a bit, so be sure you have lots of people to eat it up.

CHICKEN RICE CASSEROLE

1/4 cup onion
1 Tablespoon butter
1 can chicken broth
1 can (5 oz.) chunk chicken
1 cup shredded cheese
1/2 cup raw rice

Saute onion in butter. Mix remaining ingredients together.

Put in 1-1/2 quart casserole dish.

Cover & bake at 375° for 1 hour.

TUNA-BROCCOLI CASSEROLE

1 package frozen broccoli
7 oz. tuna
1 can cream of celery soup
1-1/4 cups crushed potato chips
1/2 cup milk

Cook broccoli & drain. Pour soup in greased 1-quart dish. Add milk & stir.

Add tuna. Place broccoli on top. Sprinkle with chips.

Bake at 350° for 20-25 minutes.

REUBEN CASSEROLE

1 pound sauerkraut (drained)
1 pound Kielbasa (cut up)
2 tomatoes, slices
8 ounces Swiss cheese, grated
4 tablespoons Thousand Island dressing
8 rye crackers, crumbled

Layer in a 1-1/2 quart casserole dish.

Bake at 425° for 15 minutes.

JOHNNY MARZETTI CASSEROLE

3 teaspoon oil
3/4 # mushrooms, sliced
3-1/2 cup tomato sauce
1 # elbow macaroni, cooked & drained
1 large onion, chopped
2 # ground beef
1-1/2 # shredded cheddar cheese

Saute onion in oil 3 minutes. Add mushrooms & cook 5 minutes. Add beef, stirring, breaking up clumps, until no longer red. Remove from heat & mix in tomato sauce & all but 1 cup cheese.

Transfer to greased 9x13 dish & add macaroni. Toss gently to mix. Put remaining cheese on top.

Bake, uncovered, 35-40 minutes at 350, browned & bubbling.

Serves 10-12.

My mother-in-law was THE Casserole Queen, especially with this one.

AMISH AFTER CHURCH 5-in-1 SKILLET CASSEROLE

1-1/2 # ground beef
1/2 # spaghetti, cook 10 minutes/drain
2 cup tomato juice
1 onion, chopped
2 cup peas
1 # favorite cheese

Brown beef & onions. Drain. Add tomato juice & simmer 20 minutes.

Put cooked spaghetti around edge of pan, put peas in center. Simmer another 15 minutes.

Cover with cheese & simmer until completely melted.

Susan Beckman

VEGAN SOLYANKA

3 cup mashed potatoes
1 small green cabbage, shredded
1 medium onion, chopped
1# mashed tofu
2 teaspoon oil
2 teaspoon cider vinegar
1/2 teaspoon caraway seeds
1/2 teaspoon dill seeds or dill weed
1/4 cup sunflower or pumpkin seeds
Soy milk
Salt & pepper
Paprika

Cook & mash potatoes (can use instant). Should be stiff consistency. Saute onion & cabbage in oil. Add dill, caraway, salt & pepper.

Add potatoes & cabbage mixture & mix. Spread mixture in greased 9x13 pan & sprinkle top with seeds & paprika.

Bake uncovered for 30 minutes at 350, or until top begins to brown.

8-10 servings

My friend, Jeannie, gave me this recipe during a time when I was a vegetarian. But it's actually good for anyone!

9-LAYER CASSEROLE

6 slices white bread
8 oz. mushrooms
2 teaspoon butter
6 oz. sliced Monterey Jack
3 beaten eggs
1 can cream mushroom soup
1/4 cup butter, melted
4 cup cooked chicken, cut up
8 oz. water chestnuts, coarse chop
1/2 cup mayo
4 oz. sliced American cheese
1-1/2 cup milk
1 can cream chicken soup
2/3 cup bread crumbs

Butter 13 x 9 pan; line with bread slices & sprinkle chicken over bread.

In pan, cook mushrooms in 2 teaspoon butter; with slotted spoon, spoon over chicken. Mix chestnuts & mayo, spoon over mushrooms; top with cheeses.

Mix eggs & milk; pour into dish. Mix soups; spread over cheese. Cover. Chill 3-24 hours.

Bake uncovered at 350 for 1-1/4 hours. Mix melted butter & bread crumbs. Sprinkle over casserole. Bake 10 mins. Just fits in pan.

10-12 servings

Susan Beckman

CHICKEN & BROCCOLI RICE CASSEROLE

1/2 cup each chopped onions & mushrooms
1 teaspoon butter
2 cup hot cooked rice
2 cup cooked chicken, cubes
2 cup broccoli
1 can cream mushroom soup
1/2 cup shredded cheese

Cook onions & mushrooms in butter. Stir in rice, chicken, broccoli & soup. Pour in buttered shallow 1-1/2 qt. dish. Top with cheese.

Bake @ 350 for 20-25 minutes

6 servings

ANNETTA GOOD'S YUM-A-SETTI

1 # macaroni or noodles
1 pt. peas and/or corn
3 # ground beef – 1 small onion
1 can cream celery soup
2 can cream chicken soup
2 cup sour cream or white sauce
Buttered bread crumbs
Grated cheese

Cook noodles. Brown beef with choice of seasonings & small onion. Mix with veggie & soups in buttered casserole dish.

Sprinkle with crumbs & cheese. Bake @ 325 for 1 hour.

15-20 servings

This is an Amish recipe. I don't know Annetta Good, but her Yum-A-Setti is good!

Susan Beckman

CHICKEN & WILD RICE CASSEROLE

2 whole cut-up chicken
2 cup water
1-1/2 teaspoon salt
1/2 teaspoon curry powder
1 med. onion
1/2 cup sliced celery
1 can mushrooms
1 can cream of mushroom soup
1 cup sour cream
2 pkg. Long grain & wild rice seasoned (6 oz. each)

Place chicken in kettle with water, salt, curry & celery. Simmer 1 hour. Drain & save broth for rice. Cut up chicken. Can saute celery & onion & add to mixture.

Cook rice according to package. Mix all together. Cover & bake @ 350 for 45-60 minutes

Can freeze before baking.

MACARONI-BACON CASSEROLE

1-1/2 cups macaroni
3/4 # fried bacon
1 can tomato soup
1/4 # Velveeta cheese cubes
1 medium onion
2-3 celery stalks
1/2 green pepper
2 cups tomato juice

Cook macaroni. Drain & rinse.

Fry bacon. In fat, fry onion, celery & pepper until tender, not brown. Remove from skillet.

Grease a casserole. Mix everything.

Bake 1 hour at 325.

Susan Beckman

CALIFORNIA CASSEROLE

1 # ground beef
1 onion
1 green pepper
1/4 # cheese (shred or chunks)
1/2 # macaroni
1 teaspoon Worcestershire
10 oz. tomatoes
3/4 cup tomato juice
1 can black olives
Salt & pepper

Mix well.

Bake 2 hours at 325.

JUDY'S BAKED SPAGHETTI

Spaghetti – mozzarella cheese
Large onion, some garlic
1 teaspoon chili powder
15 oz. tomato sauce
3 slices bacon, fried & cut up
1-1/2 teaspoon salt & pepper
1# ground beef
2-1/2 cups water

Brown beef, onion & garlic; add rest. Simmer 25 minutes. Break up spaghetti and lay single layer in greased casserole dish. Layer with sauce, then cheese.

Bake covered at 350 for 30 minutes. Uncover & cook 15 minutes.

My friend, Judy Leisenheimer, made this back in the 1970s & 1980s. I've been making it ever since. Thanks, Judy!!

PASTA & SPINACH CASSEROLE

3 heads fresh spinach
3 cloves garlic
2 Tablespoon oil
2 cups milk
¼ cup chopped Spanish olives
1 shallot or onion
3 oz. goat cheese
2-1/2 Tablespoon flour
3 cups cooked pasta
pepper

Steam spinach. Mince onion & garlic. Crumble goat cheese. Heat oil, add flour to form a roux. Whisk in milk & cook until thickened to make white sauce.

Grease casserole pan & ladle in some white sauce. Layer pasta, spinach, cheese, olives, onions, garlic, pepper & more white sauce (in that order). Continue until all used.

Bake covered for 15-20 minutes. Uncover & cook 5-10 minutes.

Farmhouse Cookbook

Susan Beckman

CHICKEN

Susan Beckman

CHICKEN WONDER

1 pound chicken breast
1 large onion, cut up
12 ounces Coke
1 medium clove garlic
1 Tablespoon coffee
1 Tablespoon ground cumin
1-1/2 teaspoon tomato paste
Oil

Heat oil. Cook meat until brown. Add onions & garlic; cook until soft. Add paste & stir until coated. Add coffee & stir until dark shiny brown color.

Pour in Coke & cumin. Cover & simmer 10 minutes.

Serve over rice or pasta.

POPPY SEED CHICKEN

1 boiled chicken or breasts
1 stick melted butter
1 can cream of chicken soup
1-1/2 cups crushed Ritz crackers
8 ounces sour cream
1 Tablespoon poppy seeds

Cut chick in chunks. Put in bottom of flat casserole. Mix sour cream & soup. Pour over chicken.

Mix butter, crackers & poppy seeds. Sprinkle over top.

Bake at 350° for 30 minutes.

WONDERFUL MOIST CHICKEN

1 cup mayo
1 teaspoon garlic powder
1-1/2 teaspoon seasoned salt
1/2 teaspoon pepper
4 chicken breasts

Mix together and coat chicken.

Bake at 375 for 45 minutes.

I use this as a go-to easy recipe for company.

MOO GOO GAI PEN

1 chicken breast
2 teaspoon oil
1/2 cup thin-sliced mushrooms
1 cup shredded Chinese cabbage
1/2 cup thin-slice bamboo shoots
2 cubes gingerroot, peel & crush
1/3 cup chicken broth
1 teaspoon sherry
7 oz. snow pea pods
3 water chestnuts, thin slice
2 teaspoon cornstarch with 1 teaspoon water
3/4 teaspoon salt
1/8 teaspoon sugar

Cut chicken in 2" strips. Heat oil; add mushrooms, cabbage, bamboo, ginger & stir fry 2 minutes Add broth, cover for 2-3 minutes Pour in bowl & set aside.

Heat remaining oil & stir fry chicken 2-3 minutes Add sherry. Add veggies & chestnuts. Heat until bubbling.

Mix cornstarch paste, salt & pepper, and heat until clear & thickened. Serve with rice.

CHICKEN & DUMPLINGS

4 # chicken
1 teaspoon salt
2 med potatoes, diced
1 teaspoon dried parsley
1 cup peas

DOUGH:
2 cup flour
1/2 teaspoon salt
2 eggs
2-3 teaspoon water

Cook chicken & salt in water to cover, until tender. Remove chicken from bones. Make dough.

Roll thin & cut into 1" squares. Drop in boiling broth. Add veggies & seasonings & cook covered 1 hour.

Beef or ham is good, too.

Susan Beckman

CHICKEN BREASTS SAUTÉ SEC

2 # chicken breasts
1 teaspoon lemon juice
1/4 cup flour
1 teaspoon salt
1/4 teaspoon pepper
1 teaspoon paprika
3 teaspoon butter
1 garlic, halved
1/2 cup dry white wine

Rub breasts with juice. Mix flour & spices in bag & coat chicken. Heat butter & garlic. Brown chicken. Add wine. Cover & simmer 20 minutes Uncover & cook until liquid is 1/2 cup. Remove chicken.

GOLDEN SAUCE: In saucepan mix:

1/8 teaspoon nutmeg
4 egg yolks   1 cup whipping cream   1 teaspoon parsley   1 teaspoon chives

Season with salt & pepper. Cook & stir until thick. Add 1/2 teaspoon lemon juice

HERBED CHICKEN & ORZO

8 oz. dried orzo
1-1/2 cup 1" pieces fresh green beans
1 whole roasted deli chicken
Two 5.2 oz semisoft cheese with garlic & herbs
1/2 cup milk
1-1/2 cup shredded carrots
2 teaspoon snipped Italian parsley

Preheat oven to 350. Grease 3-qt. baking dish; set aside. Cook orzo, adding beans during last 3 minutes of cooking; drain. Cut chick in 6 pieces; set aside.

In large bowl, whisk together cheese & milk until mixed. Add hot orzo; stir until coated. Stir in carrots. Spoon into baking dish. Top with chicken pieces.

Bake covered 30-40 minutes or until heated through. Let stand 5 minutes Sprinkle with parsley.

Susan Beckman

CHICKEN & BROCCOLI ALFREDO

8 oz. linguine
1 cup fresh or frozen broccoli
2 teaspoon butter
1 # chicken breasts, cut in 1-1/2" pieces
1 can cream of mushroom soup
1/2 cup milk
1/2 cup grated Parmesan cheese
1/4 teaspoon pepper

Prepare linguine. Add broccoli during last 4 minutes Drain linguine & broccoli.

Heat butter in skillet over med/high heat. Add chicken & cook until well browned, stirring often. Stir soup, milk, cheese, pepper & linguine mix into skillet.

Cook until mixture is hot and bubbling. Serve with additional Parmesan.

CHICKEN FRIED STEAK

Beef, thin
Flour – salt & pepper
Milk
Crushed saltine crackers
Egg & milk

Pound thin beef. Coat in flour & fry; salt & pepper. Can bread with crackers; egg with 2-4 teaspoon milk.

Gravy: Sift flour in hot fat, stir constantly; cook 1-2 minutes over med/high heat. Pour milk in quickly; turn heat down & stir (1/4 cup fat = 3-4 cup milk)

Susan Beckman

CHICKEN CORDON BLEU

1/2 oz. ham & swiss cheese
1 chicken breast, pounded
2-1/4 teaspoon bread crumbs
1 teaspoon butter

Melt 1/2 butter; add chicken & cook briefly on each side. Transfer to plate & top with ham & cheese. Start at narrow end, roll up. Secure with toothpick & put in baking dish; set aside.

Preheat oven 400. In same skillet, melt butter; add crumbs & stir. Sprinkle over chicken & bake until cheese melts, 2-3 minutes Remove toothpick & serve.

1 serving

PECAN CHICKEN TENDERS SALAD

Oil – Salt & pepper
2 # chicken tenders
1 cup flour
2 eggs, beaten with
    water or milk
1 cup plain bread crumbs
1 cup pecans,
    finely chopped
1/2 teaspoon nutmeg
1 orange, zested

Dressing:
1/4 cup maple syrup
1/4 cup tangy BBQ sauce
1 navel orange, juiced
1/4 cup olive oil
Salt & pepper
3 romaine hearts, chopped
6 radishes, thinly sliced
6 scallions, chopped on angle

Heat 2" oil over med/high heat. Season chicken with salt & pepper. Set out 3 shallow dishes. Place flour in 1 dish, eggs in 2nd, bread crumbs, pecans, nutmeg & zest in 3rd. coat tenders in batches in flour, then egg, then bread crumbs. Fry tenders 6-7 minutes Drain tenders on paper towels.

Mix syrup, BBQ sauce & orange juice in bowl. Whisk in oil with salt & pepper. Mix romaine, radishes & scallions in lg. Bowl. Toss with 3/4 of dressing.

Top salad with chicken tenders & drizzle remaining dressing over top.

Susan Beckman

ST. STEPHAN'S CHICKEN PAPRIKASH

2 chickens, cut up
Large onion, chopped
2 teaspoon paprika
1-2/ to 2 cup water
1 stick butter
Sour cream

Bring to simmer onion, paprika, water and butter in lg. Oven-proof skillet. Add chicken. Turn to coat. Bake at 350-400 uncovered for 1 hour.

Remove chicken & keep warm. Add 2 teaspoon flour to hot sauce, stir, and add 1 cup or more sour cream; mix. Add cooked noodles or spätzle. Serve with chicken.

Grandma Fitzie got this recipe from St. Stephan's Church in Toledo, Ohio. Of course it's a Hungarian recipe, but I use chicken breasts instead of bone-in chicken. I actually could eat just the spätzle with the sauce.

DEVILED CHICKEN

1/3 cup flour
1/2 teaspoon salt
1/2 teaspoon garlic salt
1/2 teaspoon pepper
1/2 teaspoon dry mustard
1/2 teaspoon paprika
1/4 teaspoon cayenne
1 chicken, cut up
3 teaspoon shortening
1 chicken cube
1 cup boiling water
1/2 cup chili sauce
2 teaspoon lemon juice

Mix flour & spices in plastic bag. Add chicken & coat.

Brown. Reduce heat. Make broth; add chili sauce & juice; add to chicken.

Cover & simmer 40 minutes

Serve with rice.

GREEK CHICKEN

Chicken breasts
Spinach
Butter & garlic
Feta cheese
Eggs & Bread crumbs

Sauce:

2 teaspoon butter-saute mushrooms
1 teaspoon flour
1 cup white wine
1 cup chicken broth
1 teaspoon lemon juice
Cook down

Pound breasts. Saute spinach in butter & garlic. Lay on breasts. Sprinkle feta on top. Roll up & secure with toothpick.

Roll in beaten eggs, then bread crumbs. Brown & bake.

CASHEW CHICKEN

1 teaspoon cornstarch
1/2 cup chicken broth
1 teaspoon cornstarch & soy sauce
1/4 # green beans, 1/2" slant
1 lg. Carrot, 1/4" slant
2 teaspoon water
1 # chicken breast, cut matchsticks
4 teaspoon oil
1 stalk celery, thin slices
1 sm. Onion, 1/4" slices
1 clove garlic, minced
1/3 cup cashews

Mix 1 teaspoon cornstarch with broth; set aside. Mix 1 teaspoon cornstarch, soy & chicken; set aside.

Put wok on high; add 2 teaspoon oil. Add chicken, stir fry 3 minutes; remove & set aside. Add 2 teaspoon oil. Add veggies; stir fry 1 minutes Add water, cover & cook 3 minutes

Return chicken & broth. Boil & thicken 1 minutes

Susan Beckman

APRICOT CHICKEN

1 whole chicken, cut up
1 bottle Wishbone Russian
1 jar apricot preserve
1 pkg. Onion soup mix
2/3 cup water

Place chicken in dish. Mix rest for sauce. Pour 1/2 over chicken & bake at 350 for 1 hour, covered.

Uncover, turn chicken & pour remaining sauce over chicken. Cook 1 hour, uncovered.

POPPY SEED CHICKEN

1 boiled chicken or chicken breasts
1 can cream of chicken soup
8 oz. sour cream
1 stick melted butter
1-1/2 cups crushed Ritz crackers
1 teaspoon poppy seeds

Cut chicken in chunks. Put in bottom of flat casserole. Mix sour cream & soup. Pour over chicken.

Mix butter, crackers & poppy seeds. Sprinkle over top.

Bake 30 minutes at 350.

MARRAKESH CHICKEN

1 chicken, skinned & cut in quarters
1T crushed coriander or 1/2 T powdered
Handful green olives
1 teaspoon dried oregano or 1/2 teaspoon powdered
Juice of 1 lemon
1 lemon, sliced thin
3 cloves garlic, chopped
1/2 cup olive oil

Sprinkle chicken with salt & arrange in baking pan. Sprinkle with lemon juice, coriander, oregano, garlic & olives. Pour olive oil over all.

Cover with lemon slices & bake at 325 for 1 hour.

Serve over couscous or rice.

ORANGE-GLAZED CHICKEN

1/2 cup olive oil
1 teaspoon wine vinegar
1 teaspoon instant chopped onion
1 chicken, about 3 #
1/2 cup orange juice
1 teaspoon salt
1/4 teaspoon ginger or cumin

Combine oil, juice, vinegar & salt; crush instant onion with mortar & pestle or back of wooden spoon, blend with ginger or cumin. Add to juice mixture.

Marinate chicken in sauce for 1 hour or longer; baste with marinade as it cooks over charcoal or in broiler.

Makes 1 cup sauce.

Susan Beckman

SPANISH CHICKEN WITH RICE & BEANS

1 green pepper, seeded & chopped
2 garlic cloves, minced
1 cup chicken broth
1 cup quick-cooking white rice
2/3 cup kidney beans, rinsed & drained
1 onion, chopped
3/4 # chicken, cubed
2 teaspoon tomato paste
1 cup drained whole tomatoes
Pepper

Spray skillet with Pam & set over medium/high heat. Saute pepper, onion & garlic until softened. Add chicken & saute until browned.

Stir in broth & tomato paste, then add rice, tomatoes, beans & pepper. Reduce heat, cover & simmer until most of broth is absorbed, 10 minutes. Uncover & cook, stirring occasionally, 5 minutes longer.

CHICKEN BREASTS FLORENTINE

10 oz. spinach
1/4 teaspoon salt
Pepper
1/4 teaspoon dried thyme
4 teaspoon olive oil
1 garlic clove, minced
2 oz. ham, cut into strips
4 chicken breasts
1/2 cup dry white wine

Heat skillet & combine spinach, garlic & pepper. Cover & cook until spinach wilts, 2 minutes. Let cool & squeeze out excess liquid. Stir in ham & pinch of thyme. Cut long thin pocket into each breast. Stuff spinach mixture into pocket, press edges together & seal closed with toothpicks.

Heat oil in skillet, add breasts & brown, turning once or twice. Add wine, salt & remaining thyme. Reduce heat to low & simmer, covered, until chicken is cooked through, 10 minutes. Serve topped with pan juices.

Susan Beckman

FAMOUS RESTAURANT CHICKEN & DUMPLINGS

3 quarts water
One 3- to 4-pound chicken, cut up
1 small onion, sliced
1 clove garlic, peeled & quartered
1-1/2 teaspoon salt
2 stalks celery, chopped
1 bay leaf
1 teaspoon pepper
1 tablespoon lemon juice
4-6 whole parsley leaves

Bring water to boil. Add chicken and everything else, except lemon juice. Cook uncovered 2 hours; liquid will reduce by about one-third. Remove chicken from pot & set aside. Strain stock.

Put 6 cups of stock back in pot. Add salt, pepper & lemon juice. Prepare dumplings. Stir until smooth; let rest for 5-10 minutes. Roll out to ½" thickness.

Cut into ½-inch squares & drop into simmering stock. Simmer 20-30 minutes until thick. Stir often.

Tear up chicken, add to pot, and cook 5-10 minutes.

<u>Dumplings</u>
2 cups flour
1 Tablespoon baking powder
1-1/4 teaspoon salt
1 cup + 2 Tablespoons milk

Very similar to the version sold in that famous restaurant that has antiques all over the walls!

CHICKEN MARTHA

2 chickens, cut up or breasts
Biscuit mix
1 quart buttermilk
1/2 # butter

Early in the day or the night before, marinate chicken in buttermilk. Cover & let stand an hour before starting dinner, drain off buttermilk. Roll chicken in biscuit mix & set on wax paper for 1 hour.

Melt butter. When sizzling, but not brown, fry chicken, turning from time to time. Watch heat so chicken doesn't burn.

I have no idea who Martha is, but her recipe is quick and easy AND good.

Susan Beckman

COOKIES

Susan Beckman

SUGAR BAR COOKIES

2-1/2 cup flour (bread is best)
1/2 teaspoon salt
1 cup sugar
1-1/2 teaspoon sour cream
1/2 teaspoon baking powder
1/2 cup butter, softened
1 egg
1 teaspoon vanilla or almond

In medium bowl, mix flour, baking powder & salt. Set aside. In large bowl, cream together butter & sugar until light & fluffy-3 minutes. (The longer you beat, the fluffier the cookies).

Add egg & mix well. Add sour cream & flavoring. Mix well. Slowly add flour mixture & stir until well combined.

Gently press into greased 9x13 dish; spread with hands. Bake 17-20 minutes at 375, or until edges become lightly golden. Cool completely

FROSTING - SUGAR BAR COOKIES

1/2 cup butter, softened
1/4 cup half and half
Pinch salt
4 cup powdered sugar
1 teaspoon vanilla or almond
Food coloring

In medium bowl, cream butter, sugar & half and half until light and fluffy.

Stir in flavoring & salt, mix well.

Add food coloring.

Frost cookie bars evenly.

Cut into squares.

SWEET & SALTINES

40 saltine crackers
1 cup light brown sugar

Line cookie sheet with foil & crackers.

2 sticks unsalted butter
8 oz semisweet chocolate chips

In medium pan, melt butter & sugar, bring to boil. Boil 5 minutes.

Pour over crackers, covering evenly. Put in 425 oven for 5 minutes or until just bubbly. Remove & pour chocolate chips over. When chips begin to melt, spread over crackers with knife.

Put in freezer for 15-20 minutes. Break into pieces & store in airtight container.

Substitute graham crackers for sweeter snack. Use 1 stick butter for crunchier cracker.

Susan Beckman

HOLLY COOKIES

6 teaspoon butter
2-1/2 cup cornflakes
24 lg. marshmallows
green food color
1/2 teaspoon vanilla
red-hot cinnamon candies

Melt butter, marshmallows, green food coloring over low heat. Pour over flakes.

Drop by teaspoon. on wax paper. Decorate with small cinnamon candies.

Look like wreaths.

These are really cute. I have a hard time with them setting up since we moved to Florida because of the humidity. So I only make them during the Christmases when it is cooler here.

LEMON PIE COOKIES

1 cup flour
¼ cup sour cream
2 teaspoon lemon curd
6 teaspoon butter, diced & cold
½ teaspoon vanilla, divided
1/3 cup powdered sugar

Pulse flour & butter in food processor until crumbly. Add sour cream & ¼ teaspoon vanilla & pulse until comes together in a ball. Place on wax paper, cover with wax paper. Roll to ¼" thick. Chill 30 minutes. (Or use prepared pie crust)

Spread lemon curd on crust and roll up. Wrap with plastic wrap & chill 2 hours or overnight. Slice roll in ½" slices. Bake on parchment at 350 for 12-15 minutes. Let cool

Mix sugar & ¼ teaspoon vanilla. Dip tops in glaze or pour glaze over.

ONE-BOWL BROWNIES

4 squares unsweetened chocolate
2 cups sugar
1-1/2 sticks butter
1 teaspoon vanilla
1 cup flour
1 cup chopped nuts

Microwave chocolate & butter 2 minutes or until melted. Stir sugar in & blend. Mix in eggs & vanilla. Stir in flour & nuts.

Spread in greased 9 x 13 pan.

Bake at 350° (325° for glass) for 30-35 minutes.

GRAHAM CRACKER COOKIES

Graham crackers
1 cup sugar
1 stick margarine
1 stick butter
1 cup chopped nuts

Line 9 x 13 pan with foil & cover entire bottom with graham crackers in the square, not crushed. Boil margarine, butter & sugar for 3 minutes.

Pour over top of crackers & sprinkle nuts on top. Bake at 350° for 10 minutes. Cool and break up. Put in airtight container.

Grandma Fitzie made these and we thought they were the best!

AMISH PEANUT BUTTER COOKIES

1 cup peanut butter
1 teaspoon vanilla
3 cup flour
1 cup brown sugar
1 cup white sugar
2 eggs
1 cup shortening
1/2 cup pure maple syrup
2 teaspoon baking soda
1/2 teaspoon salt

In large mixing bowl, cream shortening & sugars until light & fluffy. Add eggs, vanilla, maple syrup & peanut butter. Mix well.

In medium bowl, mix flour, baking soda, & salt. Add into creamed mixture. Mix well.

Please 1 large teaspoon of dough 1" apart & flatten with fork. Bake 10 minutes at 375. Cool slightly & remove from pan.

The absolute BEST peanut butter cookies I've ever made.

FORGOTTEN COOKIES

Turn oven to 350°.

Mix: 2 egg whites & pinch cream of tartar
Beat until real stiff

Add: 2/3 cup sugar, little at a time
1 teaspoon vanilla

Fold in: 1 cup nuts
1 cup chocolate chips

Drop by teaspoon on foil-lined cookie sheet. Turn oven off & put in oven & forget until oven gets cold.

Another one of Grandma Fitzie's "keepers."

Susan Beckman

AMISH MONSTER COOKIES

2 stick butter
3 eggs
1 teaspoon vanilla
1 teaspoon corn syrup
4-1/2 cup oatmeal
1 cup white sugar
1 cup brown sugar
2 cup chocolate chips
1-1/2 cup peanut butter
2 cup M&M's, & anything else - except the kitchen sink

Cream butter & sugars. Add eggs, one at a time. Add corn syrup, baking soda & peanut butter. Mix until smooth. Add oatmeal, mix well. Add chocolate chips, mix; add M&M's & anything else.

Drop 1 teaspoon on ungreased cookie sheets. Bake 10-15 minutes at 350.

Edges should be golden brown. Let cool 3 minutes before moving.

Makes 4-1/2 dozen or more.

CLUM CHRISTMAS COOKIES

2 cups sugar
4 eggs
1 cup butter
1 cup buttermilk
1 teaspoon baking powder
2 teaspoons anise
6 cups flour

Cream sugar & butter. Add eggs. Add remaining ingredients.

Flour board heavily & work in flour with hands. Roll dough sort of thick (1/8" – 1/4). Cut out with cookie cutters.

Bake at 350° for approximately 10-13 minutes. Take out when sort of white.

The frosting for these is in the Frosting chapter.

My mom made these every Christmas. It is messy decorating them with the colored sugar. We had two neighbor girls who just moved in from Italy and couldn't speak English. My mom thought it would be nice to have them over to decorate the cookies. By the time they left that night their hands were all black from licking the colored sugar off their hands and mixing the colors. I hope they had a good time, but I'm sure their mother didn't like it when they came home!

Susan Beckman

OATMEAL CINNAMON CHIP COOKIES

1 cup butter, soft
1 cup brown sugar
1/3 cup sugar
1 teaspoon baking soda
1-2/3 cup cinnamon chips
2 eggs
1-1/2 teaspoon vanilla
1-1/2 cup flour
2-1/2 cup quick oats
3/4 cup raisins

Beat butter & sugars until creamy. Add eggs & vanilla; beat well. Mix flour & baking soda; add to butter mix, beat well. Stir in oats, cinnamon chips & raisins (batter will be stiff).

Drop heaping teaspoons on ungreased cookie sheet. Bake 10-12 minutes @ 350 or until lightly browned. Cool 1 minutes before removing. 4 doz.

BARS: Spread in lightly greased 13x9. Bake at 350 for 25-30 minutes

AMISH SUGAR COOKIES

1 cup butter, soft
1 cup sugar
2 eggs
4-1/2 cup flour
1 cup oil
1 cup powdered sugar
1 teaspoon vanilla
1 teaspoon each baking soda & cream/tartar

Beat butter, oil & sugars. Beat in eggs until well blended. Beat in vanilla. Mix flour baking soda & cream of tartar; gradually add to creamed mix.

Drop by small teaspoonfuls onto ungreased baking sheet. Bake @ 375 for 8-10 minutes or until lightly browned.

Makes 5 dozen

Susan Beckman

KOLACKY

2 12-oz. Solo filling
1-1/2 cup flour
1 cup butter
1 teaspoon milk
8 oz. cream cheese
1/2 teaspoon baking powder
1 teaspoon sugar
1 egg yolk

Sift flour & baking powder. Cream butter & cream cheese, milk & sugar. Add beaten egg yolk. Add flour mixture. Chill several hours or overnight.

Roll out to 1/8" thick & cut into squares. Put filling in center & fold over. Place on ungreased cookie sheet.

Bake @ 400 for 10-15 minutes or until slightly brown. Put powdered sugar on top.

These are Hungarian pastries. They are a lot of work, but good to make at holidays.

CARMELITAS

2 cup flour
1-1/2 cup brown sugar
1/2 teaspoon salt
2 cup (12 oz) semi-sweet chocolate
1-1/2 cup (12 oz) caramel ice cream topping
2 cup quick oatmeal
1 teaspoon baking soda
1-1/2 cup melted butter, 3 sticks
1 cup chopped pecans

In large bowl, mix flour, oats, sugar, salt & butter. Blend at low speed to form crumbs. Press half in 13x9 pan. Bake 10 minutes at 350.

Remove & sprinkle with chocolate chips & pecans. Blend caramel with 6 teaspoon flour and pour over. Sprinkle remaining crumbs on top.

Bake 15-20 minutes Chill 1-2 hours.

One of my mom's favorites! They are gooey and marvelous.

Susan Beckman

MAGIC COOKIE BARS

1/2 cup butter
1-1/2 cup graham cracker crumbs
1-1/3 cup coconut
14 oz Eagle Brand
6 oz semi-sweet chocolate chips
1 cup chopped nuts

Heat oven to 350 (325 glass). In 9x13 pan, melt butter in oven.

Sprinkle crumbs over; pour milk evenly over crumbs. Top with remaining ingredients. Press down.

Bake 25-30 minutes Cool. Chill.

CONGO SQUARES

1 cup shortening
3 eggs
3 teaspoon baking powder
1 packages chocolate chips
1 packages brown sugar
2-3/4 cup flour
1 cup nuts

Melt shortening. Add sugar & eggs. Beat well. Fold in dry ingredients.

Add nuts & chips.

Grease 15x10 pan. Bake 20-25 minutes at 350.

Susan Beckman

CHOOSY CHEESE BARS

CRUST:
1-1/4 cup flour
1/2 cup brown sugar
1/2 cup butter, softened
1 teaspoon vanilla

FILLING:
1/2 cup sugar
1 teaspoon flour
1/2 teaspoon almond extract
8 oz cream cheese, softened
1 large egg

TOPPING:
3 teaspoon each of 6 selected toppings: butterscotch, chocolate or coconut, raisins, dried fruit bits, peanut butter chips, chopped nuts, granola or crisp rice cereal.

Lightly grease 9x13 pan. Mix all crust ingredients. Press into bottom of pan. Bake until light golden brown, 12-15 minutes Cool 15 minutes In same bowl, blend all filling ingredients until smooth. Spread over cooled crust.

Sprinkle heaping teaspoon of first topping crosswise in a 1" narrow band over filling; repeat with remaining 5 toppings; making 12 bands of topping.

Bake until puffy & set, 15-20 minutes Cool before cutting. Store in fridge.

SOUR CREAM PUMPKIN BARS

1/2 cup butter, softened
1-1/3 cup sugar
1-1/2 teaspoon baking powder
1/4 teaspoon baking soda
1/4 teaspoon salt
2 eggs
1 cup canned pumpkin
1/2 cup sour cream
1/4 cup milk
1 teaspoon vanilla
1-1/2 cup flour
1/2 cup whole wheat flour
1 cup chopped nuts

Grease 15x10x1" baking pan.

In large bowl, beat butter for 30 seconds Beat in sugar, baking powder, soda & salt until combined. Add eggs, pumpkin, sour cream, milk & vanilla; beat until combined.

Add flours; beat until combined. Stir in 1 cup nuts.

Spread evenly into pan.

Bake at 350 for 25 minutes Cool & frost with the following BROWNED BUTTER FROSTING.

BROWNED BUTTER FROSTING

1/2 cup butter
3 cup powdered sugar
2 teaspoon milk
1 teaspoon vanilla

In small saucepan, heat 1/2 cup butter over low heat until melted. Continue heating until butter turns a light brown. Remove saucepan from heat & transfer butter to medium mixing bowl.

Add remaining ingredients. Beat until combined. Beat in additional milk, 1 teaspoon. At a time to make a spreadable frosting. Use immediately.

Makes 1 cup

OATY RHUBARB STREUSEL BARS

1-1/2 cup quick-cooking oats
1 cup flour
3/4 cup brown sugar
2 cup fresh or frozen rhubarb
2 teaspoons flour
1/2 teaspoon ground ginger
3/4 cup butter
1/4 cup sugar
1 teaspoon finely chopped
crystallized ginger (opt.)

Preheat oven to 350. Line 8x8x2" pan with heavy foil extended beyond edges. In large bowl stir together oats, 1 cup flour & brown sugar. Cut in butter until mixture resembles coarse crumbs. Set aside 1 cup oat mixture. Press remaining on bottom of prepared pan. Bake 25 minutes

In medium bowl stir together sugar, 2 teaspoon flour & ginger. Add rhubarb; toss to coat. Spread on hot crust. Sprinkle reserved oat mixture; press lightly. Bake 30-35 minutes until top is golden & filling is bubbly. Cool on rack.

Frost with the following GINGER ICING.

I have fond childhood memories of rhubarb. We had a patch of it in our backyard. We would pick a stalk, run in the house, wash it off, and dip it in sugar to eat!

Susan Beckman

GINGER ICING

3/4 cup powdered sugar
1/4 teaspoon ground ginger
3-4 teaspoon apricot nectar, orange juice or milk

Drizzle icing & sprinkle crystallized ginger. Lift form pan; cut into bars. Store, covered, in fridge up to 2 days.

SEEDED COOKIES

1/2 # butter
1-1/4 cup sugar
2 beaten eggs
2 teaspoon vanilla
1/4 teaspoon salt
2-1/2 teaspoon baking powder
4 cups flour
Sesame Seeds

Let butter get to room temp. Mix rest, except flour and seeds. Then add 1 cup of flour at a time until thoroughly mixed. Let sit in fridge 1/2 hour.

Take about 1/2 teaspoon dough, roll into ball, then roll into seeds, form into elongated shape.

Bake 15 minutes Check; if edges are brown, put on top shelf to brown.

SNICKERDOODLES

1 cup shortening (part butter)
1-1/2 cup sugar
2 eggs
2-3/4 cup flour
2 teaspoon cream of tartar
1 teaspoon soda
1/4 teaspoon salt
2 teaspoon sugar
2 teaspoon cinnamon

Mix shortening, sugar & eggs. Mix flour, tartar, soda & salt; blend in.

Form 1" balls. Roll in mixture of sugar & cinnamon.

Place 2" apart on ungreased sheet. Bake at 400 for 8-10 minutes

La LECHE LEAGUE OATMEAL COOKIES

3/4 cup shortening
1-1/2 cup brown sugar
1 egg
1/4 cup water
1 teaspoon vanilla

1 cup flour
1/2 cup dry milk
1 teaspoon salt
1/2 teaspoon baking soda
2 cup oats
1 cup wheat germ

Beat first 5 ingredients. Sift dry ingredients. & add to shortening mixture. Mix well. Add oats & wheat germ.

Drop by teaspoon on greased cookie sheet. Bake at 350 for 12-15 minutes

Can add nuts, raisins, dates, coconut, or chocolate chips.

Susan Beckman

BROWNIE CHIP COOKIES

1 pkg. (15 oz.) brownie mix
2 eggs
2 teaspoon oil
1/2 – 1 cup chocolate chips

Mix brownies, eggs & oil. Beat with spoon. Stir in chips.

Bake at 350 for 8-10 minutes Cookies are soft to touch.

MOLASSES OATMEAL COOKIES

1-1/4 cup flour
3/4 teaspoon baking soda
1/2 teaspoon baking powder
1/2 teaspoon salt
1 teaspoon cinnamon
1/2 teaspoon ginger
1/2 cup shortening
1/2 cup sugar
1/2 cup molasses
2 eggs
1-1/2 cup oatmeal
1 cup raisins
1 cup chopped nuts

Sift flour, soda, powder, salt & spices. Add remaining ingredients. & mix until blended.

Jumbo = 1/4 cup dough on ungreased baking sheet at 350 for 15 minutes

Small = 1 teaspoonful on ungreased baking sheet at 350 for 12 minutes

Susan Beckman

UNBAKED OATMEAL BALLS

1/4 cup butter
3/4 cup sugar
1/2 cup grated apple or pear
1-1/2 teaspoon cocoa
1/4 teaspoon salt
1-1/2 cup oats, quick
1/2 cup nuts
1/2 teaspoon vanilla

Melt butter; add sugar, apple, cocoa & salt. Boil 1 minutes Remove & add oats & vanilla.

Mix & drop by teaspoon on wax paper.

When cold, form into balls & roll in powdered sugar, if desired.

I made these quite often when my girls were little. They were very healthy.

POTATO CHIP COOKIES

1-1/2 cup flour
1/2 teaspoon salt
1 cup soft butter
2 eggs, slightly beaten
1 cup sugar
1 teaspoon vanilla
1 cup chopped almonds
2 cup crushed potato chips

Mix well & drop onto ungreased cookie sheet by teaspoon.

Bake at 375 for 8-10 minutes.

Potato chips in cookies? Grandma Fitzie made them taste so good.

PUMPKIN COOKIES

1 cup butter
1 cup sugar
1 cup pumpkin
1 egg
2 cup flour
1 teaspoon soda
2 teaspoon cinnamon
1/2 teaspoon salt
1/2 cup nuts

Mix & bake at 350 for 10-12 minutes

ICING:

3 teaspoon butter
1/2 cup brown sugar
4 teaspoon milk
3/4 teaspoon orange flavoring or vanilla
1 cup powdered sugar

GAUFLETTES

8 eggs
2 cup brown sugar
5-6 cup flour
1 # melted butter
2 cup sugar
3 teaspoon vanilla

Mix. On electric stove, cook on med/low heat about 1-1/2 to 2 minutes on each side.

These are a French cookie that look like little waffles. They are very time consuming and you must have a gauflette iron to cook them in. My mom always complained every Christmas when she made these, but she couldn't resist because they are so good.

Susan Beckman

BEST COOKIES YOU EVER ATE

2 cup butter
2 cup sugar
2 cup brown sugar
4 eggs
2 teaspoon baking soda
2 teaspoon vanilla
4 cup flour
1 teaspoon salt
2 teaspoons baking powder
24 oz. chocolate chips
8 oz. Hershey chocolate Bar, grated
3 cup chopped nuts
5 cup blended oatmeal -measure & blend to a fine powder

Cream butter & both sugars. Add eggs & vanilla.
Mix with flour, oatmeal, salt, bk. Powder & bk.
Soda. Add choc chips, grated choc & nuts.

Roll into balls & place 2" apart on ungreased
cooking sheet.

Bake at 375 for 6 minutes

Makes 112 cookies & recipe can be halved.

*This recipe has floated around family and friends
and the Internet. There is a story behind it
regarding Neiman Marcus!*

MAMAU'S CREAM WAFER COOKIES

1 cup soft butter
1/3 cup whipping cream
2 cups flour
sugar

FILLING:
1/4 cup soft butter
3/4 cup powdered Sugar
1 teaspoon vanilla
Cream until smooth & fluffy. Tint
With few drops food color. Add
Drops of water if necessary

Mix butter, cream & flour. Cover & chill.

Heat oven to 375. Roll 1/3 of dough at a time, 1/8" thick on floured surface; keep remaining dough refrigerated. Cut in 1-1/2" circles. Put on wax paper covered with sugar. Coat both sides. Put on ungreased cookie sheet. Prick with fork 4 times. Bake 7-9 minutes. Cool. Put together with filling.

My husband's grandmother, Mamau Holtzapple, made these every Christmas. They melt in your mouth.

MACAROONS

1-1/3 cup coconut
2 egg whites
1/2 teaspoon almond flavor
1/3 cup sugar
3 teaspoon flour
1/8 teaspoon salt

Mix coconut, flour & salt. Stir in egg whites & flavor.

Drop by teaspoon on lightly greased cookie sheet.

Bake 20 minutes at 325 or until edges are golden brown.

Remove immediately.

Makes 1-1/2 dozen

ANGEL WINGS

1 cup sour cream
4 egg yolks
1/2 teaspoon salt
2 cup flour

Mix sour cream & yolks; add flour to make soft dough. Knead until smooth.

Roll out very thin. Cut into diamond shape. Make slit in middle, then pull one end through the slit.

Fry in deep fat until golden brown. Drain & dust with powdered sugar.

Another one of Grandma Fitzie's favorites, but then again she always loved deep frying everything back in the day.

Susan Beckman

Farmhouse Cookbook

Susan Beckman

DESSERTS

Susan Beckman

STRAWBERRY PRETZEL DESSERT

2 cup fine crushed thin pretzel sticks (9 oz.)
1-1/2 sticks butter, room temp.
Strawberry Jell-O – 6 oz.
1 cup sugar
2 cup sliced strawberries, fresh or frozen
3 teaspoon sugar
2 cup boiling water
8 oz. cream cheese
1 cup Cool Whip
Additional Cool Whip for garnish

Mix pretzels with sugar & butter. Press into 9x13 dish for form crust. Bake 6-10 minutes until lightly browned. Cool completely.

Pour 2 cup boiling water over Jell-O. Stir & cool to room temp. Beat cream cheese, 1 cup sugar & Cool whip until combined. Spread over cooled crust.

Add strawberries to cooled Jell-O & let thicken slightly. Spread over cream cheese layer. Refrigerate until firm. Cut into squares.

Susan Beckman

AMISH BREAD PUDDING

2 cup whole milk or 1/2 & 1/2   3 eggs
2/3 cup brown sugar
3 cup French bread, in small pieces
1/4 cup butter
1 teaspoon vanilla
2 teaspoons cinnamon
1/4 teaspoon nutmeg
1/2 cup raisins (optional)

Heat milk until film forms. Mix butter in & stir until melted. Cool to lukewarm. Mix sugar, eggs, spices. Beat at med. speed 1 minutes Slowly add milk mixture. Put break in lightly greased 1-1/2 qt. casserole. Sprinkle with raisins. Pour batter on top. Bake 45-50 minutes at 350 or until set. Serve warm.

SAUCE:
1 cup whole milk, 2 teaspoon butter, 1/3 cup sugar, 1 teaspoon vanilla, 1T flour, dash salt. Bring to boil for 3-4 minutes, stirring constantly. Set aside 5 minutes, then pour on warm bread pudding.

If using sauce, use only 1/3 cup sugar in bread mix above.

> *I hate bread pudding, but I make this for my daughter, Amy, who says it is the best! And she should know - she is the judge of ALL bread puddings ever made! But she might not eat it now after seeing these ingredients.....*

PEACH COBBLER

1/2 cup oatmeal
1/4 cup dry milk
1/4 cup flour
1/2 cup brown sugar
1/2 cup butter
14 oz. peaches or apples

Drain & save syrup. Put fruit & some juice in bowl. Mix remaining ingredients. Sprinkle over fruit.

Bake at 350° for 25 minutes.

Don't know why this is called a cobbler, when it actually turns out like a crisp. My mom used to make it in a stainless steel bowl.

Susan Beckman

CRISP CHERRY SURPRISE

6 ounces cherry pie filling
1/4 cup melted butter
1 cup yellow or white cake mix
1/2 teaspoon cinnamon

Put filling into 8" skillet or pie plate. Sprinkle cake mix on top. Pour butter over top & sprinkle with cinnamon.

Bake at 400° for 30 minutes.

Quick and easy. Good enough for company. I always keep these ingredients on hand just in case I need something in a hurry.

RICE KRISPIE TREATS

1 package (10 oz. or 40 regular) marshmallows
   OR
4 cups mini-marshmallows
5 cups Rice Krispies
1/4 cup butter

Melt butter in large saucepan over low heat. Add marshmallows & stir until completely melted. Remove from heat. Add rice krispies. Stir until well coated.

Using buttered spatula or wax paper, press mixture evenly into 9 x 13 pan coated with Pam. Cut into squares when cool.

Microwave Directions

Microwave butter & marshmallows at high 2 minutes Stir to combine. Microwave at high 1 minutes longer. Stir until smooth. Add cereal. Stir until well coated. Press into pan.

Back in the 1970s my friend, Teresa Dallas, always had these. And since we were all living on Air Force pay back then, they were cheap to make!

BERRIES WITH MASCARPONE & MERINGUE

10-oz. Strawberries, quartered
1-1/4 cup blackberries
4 teaspoon sugar
1/2 cup mascarpone cheese
Cinnamon – pinch
1-1/4 cup raspberries
2/3 cup blueberries
2 teaspoon lemon juice
1/2 cup whipping cream
Meringue cookies, 4, crumbled

Toss berries, 2 teaspoon sugar & lemon juice in bowl. Let stand until juices form, tossing occasionally, about 30 minutes

Stir mascarpone in bowl to loosen. Beat cream, remaining 2 teaspoon sugar & cinnamon to soft peaks. Fold 1/4 of the cream into the mascarpone to lighten. Fold in remaining whipped cream.

Using slotted spoon, divide berries among plates. Spoon mascarpone atop berries. Sprinkle meringue cookies over top. Drizzle berry juices around the dessert & serve immediately.

6 servings

BLUEBERRY DELIGHT

1/2 cup sugar
1 stick butter
1/2 cup sugar
Blueberry pie filling
1 cup graham cracker crumbs
8-oz. Cream cheese
2 eggs

Mix sugar, graham cracker crumbs & butter. Pat in bottom of pan.

Beat together cream cheese, sugar, & eggs. Pour on first mixture. Bake 30 minutes at 350. Let cool.

Pour blueberry filling on top. Refrigerate. Serve with whipped cream on top.

Grandma Fitzie

Susan Beckman

PINEAPPLE DELIGHT

1-1/2 cup oats
1/3 teaspoon salt
1 cup brown sugar
1-1/2 cup flour
3/4 cup butter
1 teaspoon baking powder
1 cup sugar
2# crushed pineapple & juice
3-1/2 teaspoon cornstarch

Blend oats, brown sugar & baking powder. Cut in flour & butter. Press into greased 13x9 pan.

Mix sugar & pineapple. Mix with cornstarch, which has been mixed with small amount of cold water. Spread over oats.

Bake at 350 for 30 minutes

Save a few crumbs for over top before baking.

PINEAPPLE CRISP

1# crushed pineapple, undrained
1/2 cup butter
14 oz. Butter pecan cake mix

Spread pineapple in greased 13x9 pan.

Scatter cake mix over to & dot with butter.

Bake 1 hour at 350.

Serve with ice cream or heavy cream.

Susan Beckman

APPLE BROWN BETTY

2 medium apples
2 English muffins
1/2 cup brown sugar
1-1/2 teaspoon cinnamon
3/4 cup water
1/4 teaspoon nutmeg
Grated lemon rind
1/2 cup nuts
5 teaspoon melted butter

Grease 9" baking dish. Peel, core & thinly slice apples. Grind muffins in blender.

Mix crumbs, sugar & spices. Reserve 1/2 cup for topping. Add apples. Put in prepared pan. Add nuts to topping. Sprinkle over top.

Pour water over mixture & drizzle butter over all. Bake 45 minutes at 350. Top with whipped cream or ice cream.

6 servings

CINNAMON CRISP

1/2 cup butter
1-1/2 cup powdered sugar
2 pkgs. Dream Whip
2 eggs
2 cup chopped peaches
Cinnamon crackers

Layer bottom of ungreased casserole dish with whole crackers. Mix butter, eggs & sugar; beat 5 minutes & spread on crackers.

Mix Dream Whip & fold in peaches. Spread over second layer of crackers. Sprinkle cinnamon crackers/crumbs on top.

Refrigerate 24 hours.

Susan Beckman

FRUIT CRISP

4 cup cut-up fruit
1-1/2 cup sugar
3/4 cup flour
1/3 cup butter
1/2 teaspoon salt
1 cup granola
1 teaspoon cinnamon
Whipped cream

Place fruit in ungreased pan; sprinkle with salt.
Mix sugar, granola, flour & spice. Stir in butter.

Sprinkle over fruit. Bake at 350 for 40-45 minutes
Serve warm.

6 servings

RHUBARB-CHERRY CRUNCH

1 cup sugar
1/2 teaspoon almond extract
1/4 teaspoon salt
3 teaspoon cornstarch
1 cup flour
1/2 cup butter
1 cup water
1 cup oatmeal
4 cup chopped rhubarb
21 oz. Cherry pie filling
1 cup brown sugar
Ice cream/whipped cream

In saucepan, stir sugar & cornstarch together. Add water. Cook & stir until thickened & bubbly; cook & stir 1 minutes Stir in cherry pie filling & almond. Set aside.

Mix flour, oats, brown sugar & salt. Cut in butter until mixture is coarse crumbs. Press 2 cup of mixture onto bottom of greased 13x9 pan. Spoon rhubarb evenly over crust. Spread with cherry mix. Combine remaining crumbs & nuts; sprinkle on top.

Bake at 350 for 40 minutes

Susan Beckman

MINTY MALLOWS

14-oz. can condensed milk
10-oz. mint-chocolate chips
2 cup mini marshmallows
1 cup coarsely chopped nuts

Combine over hot (not boiling) water, milk and chocolate Chips. Stir until chips are melted & mixture is smooth.

In lg. Bowl, mix marshmallows & nuts. Add chocolate mixture; mix well.

Spread into foil-lined 9" square pan. Chill until firm (about 20 minutes)

FRUIT COBBLER

1/4 cup butter
1 cup sugar
1 cup flour
1/8 teaspoon salt
2 teaspoon baking powder
1/2 cup milk
2 cup fruit with 1-1/2 cup sugar

Cream butter & sugar. Mix flour, salt & baking powder & add alternately with milk to cream mix. Pour in greased 9x9x2 dish.

Drain fruit, reserve 1 cup juice. Put fruit over top; pour juice over top.

Bake @ 375 for 45 minutes Serve with cream, ice cream or whipped cream.

FRUIT: Blackberries, cherries, peaches, plums, blueberries, raspberries, apples, etc.

Susan Beckman

SOUTHERN NUT DESSERT

3 eggs
1 cup sugar
1/2 teaspoon baking powder
2 cup chopped walnuts or pecans
Fresh berries or fruit
Whipped cream

Beat eggs until light. Slowly beat in sugar & bk. Powder. Beat 5 minutes until light & lemon-colored. Mix in nuts.

Generously butter 8" pan. Pour in. smooth top evenly.

Bake at 350 for 40 minutes cool. Press dry "shell" on top down to look crumbly. Cut in squares

TINA'S CHOCOLATE GRAHAM DESSERT

Graham crackers
2 boxes vanilla pudding
12 oz. Cool Whip
Hershey syrup

Put 1/2 crackers in pan. Top with 1/2 pudding mix. Put rest of crackers & pudding.

Pour syrup on top & chill 24 hours.

Susan Beckman

IMPOSSIBLE BROWNIE PIE

4 eggs
1 bar (4 oz.) sweet chocolate, melted & cooled
1/2 cup brown sugar
1/4 cup butter, soft
1/2 cup Bisquick
1/2 cup sugar
3/4 cup nuts

Heat oven to 350. Grease pie plate. Beat all ingredients.; add nuts. Pour in plate; sprinkle with nuts.

Bake 30-35 minutes Cool 5 minutes Serve with ice cream.

INDOOR S'MORES

2/3 cup light corn syrup
2 teaspoon butter
11.5 oz chocolate chips
1 teaspoon vanilla
8 cup Golden Grahams
3 cup mini marshmallows

Grease 13x9 pan. Heat syrup, butter & chocolate Chips to boiling; stir constantly; remove from heat. Stir in vanilla.

Pour over cereal in lg. Bowl; toss quickly until coated. Fold in marshmallows 1 cup at a time.

Press in pan with waxed paper. Stand 1 hour.

When you don't have a campfire going and you have that hankering for a s'more, this is a good one to make.

Susan Beckman

OREO PIE PUDDING

1 sm. Pkg. Oreos
8 oz. cr. Cheese, room temp.
1 cup sugar
1 lg. Cool Whip
1 stick butter
1 lg. Instant chocolate pudding

Crush all oreos (save 3/4 cup for top). Melt butter; pour over crumbs in bottom of 9x13 dish.

Cream cheese until fluffy; add sugar; fold in 1 cup Cool Whip. Pour over cookies. Chill 30 minutes

Prepare pudding; pour over top. Cover with 2 cup Cool Whip. Sprinkle crumbs on top. Chill & serve.

STRAWBERRY PARFAIT

6 oz. strawberry Jell-O
1-1/2 cup hot water
1 cup sour cream
1 can (20 oz.) pineapple & juice
2 mashed bananas
2 packages, frozen strawberries

Dissolve Jell-O in water; add strawberries & pineapple, including juices. Pour 1/2 into 8x8 pan. Chill 1 hour. Spread sour cream over all.

Spoon remaining Jell-O over sour cream. Chill until set. May be served in sherbet glasses.

My mom made this so many times I think she had it memorized and could make it in her sleep.

Susan Beckman

LEMON SQUARES

1 cup flour
1/2 cup butter
1/4 cup powdered sugar

Mix & pat evenly into 8 x 8 pan. Bake 20 minutes At 350.

Beat together:

2 eggs
1 cup sugar – dash salt
1/2 teaspoon baking powder
2-1/2 teaspoon lemon juice

Pour over baked crust & return to oven for 20-25 minutes

Sprinkle with powdered sugar.

Farmhouse Cookbook

Susan Beckman

DIPS

Susan Beckman

JALAPENO POPPER DIP

6-8 slices bacon, diced & cooked
1 cup mayo
1 cup cheddar cheese, shredded
1/4 cup diced green onion
2 8-oz. cream cheese, soft
4-6 jalapenos, chopped & de-seeded
1/2 cup mozzarella, shredded

Topping:

1 cup crushed crackers (can use Ritz)
1/2 cup parmesan
1/2 stick butter, melted

Mix in bowl. Transfer to ovenproof dish. Usually to make it 1" thick.

Mix topping & sprinkle over top of dip.

Bake at 350 for 20-30 minutes or until bubbly.

DO NOT DOUBLE RECIPE.

Susan Beckman

SPINACH ARTICHOKE DIP

2 cans artichoke hearts, chopped
2 boxes frozen spinach
2 large packages shredded cheese
16 oz sour cream
Garlic
Dill
Tabasco
Spices

Put all into food processor.

Spread in 13x9 casserole dish.

Bake at 300-350 until top is slightly brown.

Serve with tortilla chips.

Tastes just as good as in the restaurants.

MARY JO'S BEAN DIP

Chopped onions, lots
Butter
Big can refried beans
4 oz cream cheese
Salsa
Colby Jack cheese, shredded

Saute onions in butter. Mix in beans & cream cheese. Cook awhile.

Mix in a little salsa & cheese. Put cheese on top & bake.

Add more cheese on top & bake until melted.

Serve with fresh-cooked flour tortilla chips.

My cousin's easy recipe. Thanks again, Mary Jo!

SLOW BALL DIP

1 large round loaf Bread
3 cans (6.5 oz each) chopped clams, drained (save juice)
1/2 teaspoon salt
Parsley
16 oz cream cheese
1 teaspoon hot pepper sauce
2 teaspoon beer
2 teaspoon Worcestershire
2 teaspoon lemon juice

Cut top from bread; hollow loaf, leaving 2" thick shell; cut removed bread in cubes. Beat cream cheese until smooth; stir in clams, 1/4 cup clam juice, onion, beer, Worcestershire, lemon juice, pepper sauce & salt.

On baking sheet make cross with 2 sheets foil, long enough to cover loaf. Pour clam mix in shell; cover with bread top. Wrap loaf with foil; bake 3 hours at 250.

Remove top; sprinkle with parsley. Surround bread with bread cubes & raw veggies. Toast bread cubes in over last 5 minutes

HOT TAMALE DIP

1 can picante dip
1# Velveeta cheese, cubed
1 large can chili without beans
1 can beef tamales – unwrapped & mashed
                          with fork

Mix & cook over low heat until tamales dissolve & cheese melts.

Stir to prevent sticking.

Serve hot with tortilla chips.

Susan Beckman

VEGIE DIP

2 cup mayo
3 teaspoon minced onion
1-1/2 teaspoon seasoned salt
6 drops Tabasco
2 cup sour cream
1 teaspoon dill
1-1/2 teaspoon Worcestershire
3 teaspoon dry parsley

Mix well & chill.

CRAB DIP

1 packages (2.4 oz) Knoor Leek soup
1/8 teaspoon hot pepper sauce
1 teaspoon lemon juice
1 cup shredded cheese
1-1/2 cup sour cream
14 oz artichoke hearts, chopped
6 oz crab meat, cooked
1 teaspoon dried dill weed

Stir soup mix, sour cream, lemon juice & hot sauce. Stir in remaining ingredients.

Cover & chill 2 hours.

Can be served hot or spooned into pastry shells.

Susan Beckman

EASY GREEK DIP

32 oz. Plain yogurt
12 oz. Roasted red peppers, drained & chopped
1/4 cup crumbled feta cheese
2 teaspoon chopped fresh dill
1 teaspoon Greek seasoning
1 small garlic clove, pressed
Pita chips

Line a fine wire-mesh strainer with coffee filter. Place strainer over a bowl. Spoon yogurt into strainer. Let stand 15 minutes Spoon yogurt into medium bowl & discard strained liquid.

Pat bell peppers with paper towels. Stir peppers, feta cheese, dill, seasoning & garlic into yogurt. Cover & chill at least 1 hour. Store in airtight container in fridge up to 3 days. Serve with pita chips.

Farmhouse Cookbook

Susan Beckman

EGGS

Susan Beckman

BACON & CHEESE OVEN OMELET

12 slices bacon
8 beaten eggs
6 slices cheese
1 cup milk

Cook bacon & chop up 4 slices. Cut cheese slices in half & put in buttered pie pan.

Beat eggs & milk. Add chopped bacon. Pour over cheese.

Bake at 350° for 30 minutes. Arrange chopped bacon on top.

Bake 10 minutes. Let stand 5 minutes.

Susan Beckman

HARD-BOILED EGGS

Cover with cold water. Pour in vinegar or salt

Bring to boil. Remove from heat. Cover for 20 minutes. Drain.

Shake to crack eggs on side of pan. Cool with cold water & peel.

This is how I USED to hard boil eggs. Now I have that egg thingie that goes in the microwave and the eggs are perfect every time.

EGG ROLLS

1 # Chinese veggies
4-1/2 oz. shrimp
2 green onions, chopped
1/4 teaspoon garlic salt
1/4 teaspoon ginger
1/4 teaspoon dry mustard
6 egg roll skins, cut in 1/2 diag.
4 cups peanut or veggie oil

Mix veggies, shrimp, onion & spices. Place 1 teaspoon in center of triangle. Fold 2 sides, roll to enclose. Fry 2 minutes Turn once.

Susan Beckman

EGGS BENEDICT

4 slices ham or Canadian bacon
1 teaspoon butter
2 English muffins, toasted & buttered
4 poached eggs
1 cup Hollandaise

Brown ham in butter; put on muffins. Top with eggs. Cover with sauce.

HOLLANDAISE SAUCE

4 egg yolks
2 teaspoon lemon juice
1/4 teaspoon salt
Pinch white pepper
1/2 cup hot melted butter

Blend yolks, juice, salt & pepper in blender 1/2 minutes Continue at high speed, adding butter drop by drop – as thickens, add in thin, slow stream.

Susan Beckman

EGGS WITH CELERY SAUCE

12 hard-boiled eggs, 1/4 lengthwise
1/2 cup celery, chopped
1/4 cup pimiento, chopped
1/3 cup saltine crumbs
7 teaspoon butter
2 oz. blue cheese
1/2 cup Sprite
2-1/2 cups milk
1 teaspoon salt
6 teaspoon flour

Melt butter in pan. Blend in flour & salt. Pour in Sprite & milk. Cook, stir constantly, until thick. Add cheese, pimiento, & celery.

Put eggs in 7 x 12 dish. Put sauce on top. Melt remaining tablespoon of butter & mix with cracker crumbs. Sprinkle around edge of dish.

Bake 45 minutes at 325.

MUSHROOM FRITTATA

6 eggs, beaten
1/4 teaspoon pepper
1 teaspoon olive oil
1 cup sliced mushrooms
1/2 teaspoon salt
1/4 teaspoon dried oregano
1 onion, chopped

Whisk together eggs, salt, pepper & oregano.

Heat oil in skillet, then add onion & mushrooms. Saute until onions are golden & mushrooms browned. Pour eggs over veggies & stir quickly just until combined. Reduce heat to low, cover & cook until eggs are set, 10-13 minutes.

Loosen edge of frittata with turner or knife. Invert onto a plate & serve.

Susan Beckman

Farmhouse Cookbook

Susan Beckman

FROSTINGS

Susan Beckman

FROSTING FOR RED VELVET CAKE

1 stick butter
1 cup sugar
1/2 cup Crisco
3 Tablespoons flour
1 teaspoon vanilla
2/3 cup milk

Mix butter, Crisco & sugar. Add flour, one tablespoon at a time. Then add milk at room temperature. Add vanilla. Mix well.

Susan Beckman

CLUM CHRISTMAS COOKIE FROSTING

1 box (4 cups) powdered sugar
5-6 tablespoons pet milk, add more if needed
2 eggs whites
2 tablespoons melted butter
1/2 teaspoon anise

Mix & frost.

MAMAU'S FROSTING

1 cup sugar
Pinch salt
1/3 cup boiling water
1/8 teaspoon cream of tartar
1 egg white
1 teaspoon vanilla

Put in double boiler. Beat 7 minutes.

Frost angel food cake.

Susan Beckman

HAM

Susan Beckman

HAM BAKE

1 pound spaghetti
1 teaspoon parsley
1 tablespoon onion flakes
2 cups cubed ham
2 cans cream mushroom soup
1 teaspoon Worcestershire
1-3/4 cups milk
2 cups grated cheese

Break spaghetti into 2" & cook in boiling water; drain well. Toss with soup, parsley, onion, Worcestershire & milk. Spread on bottom of 3-quart greased casserole dish.

Layer ham & cheese on top. Cover & bake at 375° for 20 minutes. Uncover & bake 10-15 minutes.

COLCANNON

3 # potatoes, scrubbed
1-1/4 cup hot milk
1 head cabbage, finely shredded
4 scallions, finely chopped
2 sticks butter
Pepper
1 # ham or bacon
Parsley, chopped, for garnish

Steam potatoes in skins for 30 minutes Peel, then chop with knife before mashing. Add 1 stick butter, then gradually add hot milk, stirring all the time. Season with pepper.

Boil cabbage in unsalted water until it turns darker color. Add 2 teaspoon butter to tenderize it. Cover with lid for 2 minutes Drain thoroughly before returning to pan. Chop into small pieces. Chop ham into small pieces.

Add cabbage, scallions & ham to mashed potatoes, stirring them in gently. Serve in individual soup plates. Make indentation on top by swirling wooden spoon. Put 1 teaspoon butter into each indentation. Sprinkle with parsley.

GOLDEN GLAZE HAM

10 oz. apple jelly
1 teaspoon lemon juice
1/2 teaspoon cinnamon
Dash nutmeg

Mix in saucepan & heat until jelly melts.

Spoon over ham last 30 minutes

Susan Beckman

HAM LOAF

1-1/4 # ground ham
1 # ground pork
3/4 cup bread crumbs or wheat germ
1/4 cup brewer's yeast (optional)
1/3 cup onions
1 teaspoon dry mustard
2 eggs
1 cup milk

Mix & put in 9 x 5x3 greased dish.

Bake 1-1/2 hours at 350. Remove & set 5 minutes

Sauce:
1 cup mayo
2 teaspoon mustard
1 teaspoon horseradish
2 cup heavy cream, whipped
dash salt
1 teaspoon horseradish

CROCK POT
HAM & SCALLOPED POTATOES

6-8 slices ham
8-10 potatoes, thin sliced
2 onions, thin sliced
1 cup grated cheese
Cream celery or mushroom soup
Paprika

Toss potatoes in 1/2 teaspoon cream of tartar & 1 cup water. Drain. Put 1/2 ham, potatoes & onions in crock pot. Sprinkle with salt & pepper, then cheese. Repeat with rest.

Spoon soup over top Sprinkle with paprika.

Cover & cook on low 8-10 hours or high 4 hours

Susan Beckman

GLAZED HAM LOAF

1 # each ground pork, ham, beef
1-1/2 teaspoon salt
1 cup bread crumbs
1 cup milk
1 # grated Swiss cheese
2 eggs

Mix ingredients well. Put in roasting pan & shape into loaf.

Bake 1-1/2 hours at 350. Mix glazed ingredients & pour over. Bake additional 1/2 hour.

Glaze:
3/4 cup brown sugar
1 teaspoon mustard
1/2 teaspoon paprika
1/4 cup vinegar

Farmhouse Cookbook

Susan Beckman

JELLIES

&

JAMS

Susan Beckman

STRAWBERRY JAM

2 # fresh strawberries
4 cup sugar
1/4 cup lemon juice

Crush strawberries to make 4 cup In pan mix ingredients. Stir over low heat until sugar dissolves. Increase heat to high & bring to full rolling boil.

Boil, stirring often, until mixture reaches 220º. Can test by putting on cold plate, put in freezer for 1 minute, and then check consistency.

Fill jars, leaving 1/4 – 1/2" head space & seal. Process in water bath 10 minutes.

Susan Beckman

PLUM JAM

2-1/2 # plums
3-1/2 cup sugar

Rinse plums & remove pits. Finely chop to make 4 cups. Stir in sugar. Let stand 1 hour. Bring to boil over med. heat, stir frequently.

Continue cooking 20 minutes or until thickened. Makes four 1/2 pints. Process upside down 5 minutes

LEMON-HONEY JELLY

3/4 cup lemon juice
2-1/2 cup honey
1/2 cup liquid pectin

Mix juice & honey; bring carefully to full rolling boil. Add pectin. Bring just to boil. Stir constantly.

Pour in jars & seal upside down 5 minutes

Susan Beckman

Farmhouse Cookbook

Susan Beckman

MAIN COURSES

Susan Beckman

GB SLOP

1 ring smoked kielbasa
4 large potatoes, cubed 1/2" x 1/2"
1 can corn, drained
1 can peas, drained
1 medium onion, chopped
Garlic, diced
Catsup
Salt & pepper

Heat a big dollop of coconut oil (or oil of your choice) on high heat. Saute onions and garlic 1-2 minutes. Do NOT overcook. Add potatoes. Stir constantly for a few minutes.

Cut kielbasa slices on an angle and add. Stir constantly for a few minutes longer. When potatoes are cooked, add corn & peas. Turn heat to medium. DO NOT LET IT STICK. If it gets dry, add 3-4 tablespoons butter. Coat with catsup, about 1 to 1-1/2 cups. Put lid on and cook about 10 minutes. Monitor constantly. Stir. Put lid back on and cook about another 10 minutes.

My husband, Greg Beckman (GB), made up this recipe when we first got married. It has become a favorite in our family. He now is teaching our grandchildren how to cook it.

Susan Beckman

HUNGARIAN GOULASH

2 pounds stew meat, cubed
2 bay leaves
1 cup chopped onion
1/4 cup flour
3 teaspoons paprika
1/4 teaspoon pepper
1 clove minced garlic
1 teaspoon salt
1/4 cup shortening
1 cup sour cream
1 can (1 #) tomatoes
1/4 teaspoon thyme

Brown meat in shortening. Reduce heat & add onion & garlic. Cook until onion is tender, but not brown.

Blend in dry ingredients & add tomatoes. Cover & simmer, stir occasionally until meat is tender, 1 to 1-1/2 hours.

Stir often towards end of cooking. Stir in sour cream. Serve at once over buttered noodles.

8 servings

STROGANOFF

1 pound ground beef
3/4 teaspoon salt
1 medium onion, chopped
1/4 teaspoon pepper
1 clove garlic, minced
1 cup water
3 Tablespoons flour
1 cup sour cream
1 teaspoon beef bouillon
4 ounces mushrooms
Noodles, rice, or mashed potatoes

Cook meat, onion & garlic. Drain. Mix in flour, bouillon, salt & pepper, and mushrooms.

Stir in water and boil. Reduce heat; cover & simmer 10 minutes.

Stir in sour cream & heat.

One of my favorites from my childhood.

Susan Beckman

CAMPFIRE KITCHEN

1/2 cup ground beef
2 slices onion
1/4 cup chopped cabbage
1/2 carrot, grated
1 slice green pepper
1 potato, 1/4" slices
1/2 celery stalk, chopped
Salt & pepper
2 Tablespoons cream soup
1 Tablespoon water

Shape meat into one patty. Place onion on foil. Add meat; season. Add green pepper, celery & cabbage. Top with carrot & potato.

Add soup & water. Wrap tightly. Grill 1 hour OR bake 1 hour at 350°.

1 serving

BOILED DINNER

2 # beef brisket
1 turnip, cubed
2 small onions
1/2 cabbage, wedges
4 carrots
Horseradish sauce
2 potatoes, halved or quartered

Put beef in kettle and cover with hot water. Cover tightly & simmer 2-1/2 to 3 hours. Remove meat.

Add veggies, except cabbage. Cover & cook 15 minutes. Add cabbage & cook 10 minutes.

Serve with horseradish sauce.

Susan Beckman

STEAK SUPPER IN FOIL

1-1/2 pound roast
1 dry onion soup mix
1 can cream of mushroom soup
2 Tablespoons water
2 stalks celery, cut in 2" pieces
3 carrots, quartered
3 medium potatoes, peeled & quartered

Put large foil in baking pan. Place meat on foil. Mix soups & spread on meat. Put veggies on top. Sprinkle with water.

Fold foil over & seal. Cook 1-1/2 hours at 450°.

SHIPWRECK

2 onions
1 cup diced celery
2 potatoes
1 cup carrots
1 pound ground beef
1 can tomato soup
1/2 cup uncooked rice
1 cup boiling water

Slice onions & potatoes. Butter casserole dish & layer with onions, potatoes, beef, rice, celery & carrots; adding salt, pepper & paprika.

Add soup & water. Cover & bake at 250° to 300° for 3-4 hours.

Susan Beckman

CALIFORNIA TACOS

2 pounds ground beef
2 packages Fritos
1 envelope taco seasoning
1 can chili beans (optional)
Tomatoes, lettuce (chopped)
Catalina French dressing
Onions, cheese (chopped)

Brown meat & add beans & seasoning. Simmer 1 hour.

Put Fritos on plate. Add meat. Then top with tomatoes, lettuce, onions & cheese.

Pour dressing over all.

Another recipe from Teresa Dallas during our Air Force days. I still make this.

SHEPHERD'S PIE

1-1/2 # ground beef
1 packet onion soup mix
1 teaspoon garlic powder
1/2 teaspoon pepper
4 cup prepared mashed potatoes
1 onion, chopped
18 oz. jar beef gravy
16 oz. mixed veggies, thawed
Paprika

Fry beef & onion. Drain liquid. Add soup mix, gravy, garlic powder & pepper. Mix well. Stir in veggies.

Place in 2-quart greased casserole dish. Spread mashed potatoes over top & sprinkle with paprika.

Bake 30-35 minutes at 350.

I've tried many of these shepherd pie recipes, but this one is the best.

Susan Beckman

PASTY

1-1/4 # beef, coarsely ground
1/4 cup rutabaga, diced big
4 medium potatoes, diced big
1 carrot, diced big
1 large onion, chopped
Salt & pepper
Butter

Mix all, except salt & pepper. Roll dough out to oval-rectangle shape, about 8 x 11. Put mixture on bottom side of dough. Sprinkle with salt & pepper. Dot with butter. Lightly wet edges with water. Fold over in half-moon shape & seal edges. Cut small slits in top.

Can use pork, beef, etc.

Bake at 375° for 40-45 minutes. Then reduce to 350° for 15 minutes.

Must be topped with ketchup!

DOUGH:
1/2 block lard (1 cup)
3 cups flour
1 tablespoon salt
1/2 – 3/4 cup COLD water, but not ice cold

From my Finnish Yooper friend, Sandi Longhini. She had to make a trip to Florida to teach me how to make these the correct way! Thanks, Sandi!

HISTORY OF THE PASTY

The famous pasty was brought here by the copper and iron miners from Cornwall, England. The Cornish miners and their wives are properly given credit for bringing the pasty to the Upper Peninsula of Michigan in the early 1850s when both the copper and iron mines were first being opened.

The original pasty that came over in the 1850s from England, along with the miners, was hearty and hot. It was a hand-held (no dish) complete meal for miners who had no time to come above ground for lunch.

Some miners reheated their pasties underground; others kept them at body warm in a chest pocket. Another way of warming a pasty while underground in a mine was to set it on a shovel and hold the pasty up to the light of a lantern.

Susan Beckman

IMPOSSIBLE LASAGNE PIE

1 pound ground beef
1 teaspoon oregano
1/2 cup small-curd cottage cheese
1/4 cup Parmesan
1/2 teaspoon basil
1 cup milk
6 oz. tomato paste
2/3 cup Bisquick
1 cup mozzarella, shredded
2 eggs

Grease pie plate. Cook beef & drain. Add oregano, basil, tomato paste & 1/2 cup mozzarella. Layer cottage cheese & Parmesan cheese in plate. Spoon beef over top. Beat milk, eggs & Bisquick until smooth. Pour in plate.

Bake at 400° for 30-35 minutes. Sprinkle with remaining cheese. Cool 5 minutes.

IMPOSSIBLE TACO PIE

1 pound ground beef
3/4 cup Bisquick
1/2 cup chopped onion
3 eggs
1 envelope taco seasoning
2 tomatoes
1-1/4 cup milk
1 cup cheese

Grease a quiche dish or pie plate. Cook beef & onion; drain. Add seasoning. Spread in plate.

Beat milk, Bisquick & eggs until smooth. Pour into plate.

Bake at 400° for 25 minutes. Top with tomatoes & cheese. Bake 8-10 minutes longer. Cool 5 minutes.

Top with sour cream in center, chopped lettuce around edges & tomatoes in between.

Susan Beckman

IMPOSSIBLE QUESADILLA PIE

8 oz. chilies
4 cup cheese
2 cup milk
1 cup Bisquick
4 eggs

Heat oven to 425. Grease pie plate. Sprinkle chilies & cheese in plate. Beat remaining ingredients. until smooth. Pour in plate.

Bake 25-30 minutes Cool 10 minutes Serve with sour cream & guacamole.

SKILLET-STYLE LASAGNA

6 lasagna noodles, broken into 2-3"
12 oz. bulk Italian sausage
1/2 cup chopped onion
1 med. zucchini, coarsely shredded
24-oz. jar marinara sauce
1 cup ricotta cheese (1/2 of 15 oz.)
3/4 cup shredded mozzarella
2 teaspoon parmesan

Cook pasta according to directions. Drain thoroughly. In a 10" skillet cook sausage & onion over med. heat until no longer pink, stirring to break up sausage. Add zucchini; cook & stir for 1 minute. Drain off fat. Remove meat from skillet.

In same skillet, arrange half of noodles. Cover with half of marinara sauce. Spoon meat over sauce. Spoon ricotta in mounds atop meat & sprinkle with 1/4 cup mozzarella.

Arrange remaining noodles atop cheese. Top with remaining marinara sauce & mozzarella. Sprinkle with Parmesan cheese.

Cook, covered, over med. heat about 10 minutes or until heated through & cheese is melted. Remove from heat. Let stand uncovered 5 minutes

SKILLET MACARONI DINNER

2 teaspoon oil
1-1/2 # gr. Beef
2 med. onions, chopped
28 oz. tomatoes
12 oz. corn
1 cup macaroni
1 teaspoon chili powder
2 teaspoon garlic salt
3-1/2 oz. black olives
4 oz (1 cup) shredded cheese

Cook beef in oil. Add onions, tomatoes, & corn with liquid & macaroni; heat to boiling.

Reduce heat to med/low; cover & cook 20-30 min, stirring occasionally.

Stir in chili powder, garlic salt & olives; sprinkle with cheese and heat, covered, 5 minutes

JIFFY GOULASH

2 teaspoon butter
1-1/2 cup chopped onion
3/4 # cooked beef
1 # tomatoes
1 bouillon cube
4 teaspoon paprika
1/2 teaspoon marjoram
1 bay leaf, crushed
1/8 teaspoon garlic powder
8 oz. noodles
1 teaspoon butter
1 teaspoon poppy seed
1/2 cup sour cream
Dash paprika

Melt butter & saute onions. Stir in beef, tomatoes, bouillon, paprika, marjoram, bay, and garlic. Simmer 15 minutes

Cook noodles. Add butter & poppy seeds.

Stir in meat with sour cream.

Susan Beckman

FRITTATA

2 teaspoon olive oil
1 small onion, minced
1/2 teaspoon salt
1/4 teaspoon pepper
1/4 teaspoon each thyme & rosemary
1 small zucchini, sliced
1 small green pepper
4 slices mozzarella
1 teaspoon melted butter
1 small clove garlic, minced
1/2 teaspoon each basil & oregano
6 mushrooms, sliced
1 small bunch spinach, chopped
5 large eggs, well beaten
1/4 cup parmesan

Cook onion & garlic with salt & herbs in oil & butter, 5-8 minutes. Add remaining veggies & cook quickly until tender, 8-10 minutes.

Turn heat way up and pour in beaten eggs. Cook for several minutes, lifting edges & letting uncooked egg flow underneath cooked egg. Turn heat back to medium. As soon as egg is set, place mozzarella on top & sprinkle with parmesan.

Place in oven at 350 for 12-15 minutes until firm & cheese is melted.

Remove & serve in wedges/hot or room temp. Cool wedges make sandwich fillings with fresh spinach & mayo.

PAPRIKASH BURGONYA

2 medium onions, peeled & chopped
3 teaspoon shortening
1-2 teaspoon paprika
6 medium potatoes, peeled & cubed
2 cloves garlic, crushed
1/4 teaspoon caraway seed
Salt & pepper, to taste
1 cup sour cream at room temp.

In saucepan, saute onions & garlic in hot shortening until tender. Stir in caraway seeds, paprika, salt & pepper; cook 1 minute.

Add potatoes & enough water to barely cover. Cook slowly, covered, for 20 minutes or until potatoes are tender. Stir in sour cream, leave on low heat until hot.

Can add tomatoes & green peppers or sliced smoked sausage for substantial meal dish.

Susan Beckman

TOMATO TART

1/2 packages (15-oz) refrigerated pie crusts
1/2 teaspoon olive oil
4 large tomatoes
1/4 teaspoon pepper
1-1/2 cup fontina cheese, shredded
1 garlic bulb
1/2 teaspoon salt

Press refrigerated pie crust on bottom & up sides of square 9" tart pan. Bake 9 minutes at 450 or until lightly browned; set aside.

Cut off pointed end of garlic bulb. Place garlic on foil & drizzle with olive oil. Fold foil to seal. Bake 30 minutes at 425; cool. Squeeze pulp from garlic cloves into bottom of baked pie crust.

Sprinkle 1/2 cup cheese over garlic.

Slice tomatoes & sprinkle evenly with salt & pepper. Place on folded paper towels & let stand 10 minutes Arrange tomato slices over cheese. Sprinkle with remaining 1 cup cheese.

Bake 45 minutes at 350 or until lightly browned.

SPAGHETTI PIE

6 oz. spaghetti
1/3 cup Parmesan
1 cup cottage cheese
1/2 cup chopped onion
8 oz. tomatoes
1 teaspoon sugar
1/2 teaspoon garlic salt
2 teaspoon butter
2 eggs
1 # ground beef
1/4 cup chopped green pepper
6 oz. tomato paste
1/2 cup mozzarella
1 teaspoon oregano

Cook spaghetti; stir in butter, Parmesan & eggs. Form into crust in buttered 10" pie plate. Spread cottage cheese over crust. Brown beef, onion & pepper. Stir in tomatoes, paste, sugar, oregano & garlic salt. Put on crust.

Bake uncovered @ 350 for 35-45 minutes Sprinkle mozzarella on top & bake 5 minutes

TACO PIE

1 pkg. Crescent rolls
2 cup Fritos, crumbled
1 # ground beef
Taco sauce
1 cup sour cream
American cheese slices

Spread rolls in pie dish as crust. Layer 1 cup Fritos, browned meat with taco sauce, sour cream & cheese & another cup Fritos.

Bake @ 350 for 30 minutes

SUMMER PIZZA

2 pkg. Crescent rolls
16 oz. cream cheese
2/3 cup mayo
1 teaspoon dill
1 teaspoon onion, minced
Veggies, cut up

Grease 10 x 15 pan. Put down crescent rolls, pressing seams together. Bake at 400 for 10 minutes.

Mix next 4 ingredients & spread on cooled dough.

Top with veggies. Chill.

Susan Beckman

SAUSAGE & SPINACH PIE

1 # sausage
2-10 oz. frozen chopped spinach, thawed & drained
1/2 teaspoon salt
1/8 teaspoon pepper
1/8 teaspoon garlic powder
6 eggs
2/3 cup ricotta cheese
2 cups shredded mozzarella
Pastry for 2-crust pie
1 teaspoon water

Brown sausage; drain. Separate one of the eggs. Set yolk aside. Mix remaining eggs, egg white, spinach, cheese, salt, garlic powder & pepper. Stir in sausage.

Roll out pastry for top & bottom crusts. Line 9" or 10" pie plate. Transfer sausage mix to pie crust. Place top crust over filling, cutting slits for steam.

Flute edges. Can cut decorative shapes from remaining crust and place on top. Mix yolk & water. Brush over crust.

Bake at 375 for 1-1/4 hours or until crust is golden & filling set. Cool 10 minutes.

Serves 10-12

Farmhouse Cookbook

Susan Beckman

PASTA

Susan Beckman

SUSAN'S MEDITERRANEAN PASTA

Penne pasta
Spinach
Sun-dried tomatoes
Olive oil
Roasted garlic
Pine nuts
Feta cheese

Cook pasta. Toss with remaining ingredients & serve!

One of my own made-up recipes!

Susan Beckman

LEMON-GARLIC SPAGHETTI

2 tablespoons butter
3 lemons, juiced & zested
2 tablespoons olive oil
1 bunch broccoli, cut florets
5-6 cloves garlic
1 cup milk
1/2 cup onions, chopped
1 teaspoon basil

Saute garlic, onions & basil in butter & oil. Cook spaghetti & drain.

Mix all together & serve.

Optional: Can juice broccoli stalks & milk in blender.

MAMAU'S NOODLES

1 dozen egg yolks
4 cups flour
Salt
Water
Chicken broth

Mix yolks, flour & salt together. Add a little bit of water at a time. Dough will be stiff.

Roll thinner than pie crust. Let partially dry. Roll up & slice noodles about 1/4" to 1/2" wide. Let dry. Freeze in baggies.

To use: Cook in boiling water for about 15 minutes. Drain & add butter and chicken broth. Spoon over mashed potatoes.

My husband's grandmother always made noodles and had them in the freezer. His family would serve them over mashed potatoes! That was new to me when I joined their family, but they have now become our family favorite.

BAKED MACARONI WITH ZUCCHINI & 3 CHEESES

1 # elbow macaroni
1 teaspoon olive oil
6 oz. mushrooms – 1/8"
1 red pepper – 1/2"
4 cup cold milk
1/4 teaspoon nutmeg
1 teaspoon Worcestershire
6 oz. sharp cheese, shredded
1/2 cup Parmesan – 1-1/2 oz.

1/2 stick butter
2 med. zucchini – 1/8"
1 large onion,
　coarse chopped
2 cloves garlic,
　fine chopped
1/4 cup flour
1 teaspoon salt
1/2 cup sour cream
3 oz. Swiss, shredded

Cook macaroni 8 min; drain; set aside. Heat 2 teaspoon butter with oil in large skillet over med heat. Add zucchini & mushrooms, saute 5 minutes Transfer to plate & set aside. Add remaining butter to skilled & add onion, pepper & garlic; saute until veggies are softened but not brown, 8 minutes.

Sprinkle flour over veggies in skillet; stir with wooden spoon. If too dry, add more butter. Cook 4 minutes Stir in milk until smooth. Bring to boil. Reduce to low. Add salt & nutmeg; simmer 5 minutes

Remove from heat & stir in sour cream, Worcestershire, & red pepper seasoning. In pot used to cook macaroni, toss together drained macaroni, reserved zucchini mix & sauce.

Butter 13x9x2 dish. Mix cheddar & swiss; set aside 1/4 cup Add remaining cheese mix to macaroni. Spoon in dish. Mix reserved 1/4 cup cheese with Parmesan; sprinkle over macaroni. Cover & fridge if making ahead. Bake uncovered @ 400 for 45 minutes until crusty. Can run under broiler 45 seconds, if desired.

DOUBLE-CHEESE MACARONI & CHEESE

8 oz macaroni, cook & drain
1-1/2 cup shredded sharp cheese
12 oz. cottage cheese
1/4 cup butter
1/4 cup flour
2 cups milk
1/2 teaspoon salt
1/8 teaspoon white pepper
1/2 cup bread crumbs
2 teaspoon melted butter

Alternate layers of macaroni & cheeses in 2-qt. baking dish, begin with macaroni & end with cheese. Melt 1/4 cup butter; stir in flour. Blend in milk. Heat to boil. Cook until thick. Add salt & pepper. Pour over macaroni & cheese. Mix crumbs with butter. Sprinkle over.

Can cover & refrigerate. Bake @ 375 for 30-35 minutes If refrigerated, add 10 minutes.

Susan Beckman

STUFFED SHELLS

2 # ricotta
1 # mozzarella
6 eggs
Garlic powder – oregano
2 lg. Jars spaghetti sauce
2 boxes shells
1/2 # grated brick cheese
1/2 cup Romano cheese
1/4 cup parsley

Boil shells. Mix other ingredients, except sauce & mozzarella. Stuff shells. Line pan with sauce.

Place shells on sauce & cover with sauce. Sprinkle mozzarella on top. Cover with foil.

Bake @ 350 for 20 minutes.

Makes two 13x9 pans

MANICOTTI

1/2 # ground beef
1 clove crushed garlic
1 cup (8 oz.) cottage cheese
4 oz. shredded mozzarella
1/2 teaspoon salt
Parmesan
1/2 cup mayo
8 manicotti, cooked & drained
16 oz. spaghetti Sauce
1/2 teaspoon oregano

Brown beef & garlic; blend cottage & mozzarella, salt & mayo into beef. Fill each manicotti with 1/4 cup filling. Put in baking dish. Sprinkle with remaining filling. Cover with sauce. Sprinkle with oregano & Parmesan. Cover with foil.

Bake @ 325 for 15 minutes Uncover & bake 10 minutes longer.

Susan Beckman

LASAGNE

1 # ground beef
2 cloves garlic, minced
2 cans (8 oz.) tomato sauce
1/2 teaspoon salt
1/4 teaspoon pepper
1/2 teaspoon oregano

Cook meat & garlic. Stir in remaining ingredients. Cover & simmer 20 minutes

8 oz. lasagne noodles
12 oz. cottage cheese
2 cup mozzarella, shredded
1/3 cup Parmesan

Cook noodles.

Heat oven to 350. In ungreased 13x9x2 dish, layer half each of noodles, meat, cottage cheese & mozzarella. Sprinkle Parmesan on top

Bake uncovered for 40 minutes.

VEGIE LO MEIN

1 # mushrooms
1/2 # pea pods
4 celery stalks
1 sm. Bunch green onions
1 large red pepper
1/4 cup soy sauce
1 teaspoon dry sherry
1 teaspoon cornstarch
1 envelope chicken broth
8 oz. linguine
1 # bean sprouts
1/4 cup roasted unsalted peanuts

Cut mushrooms into quarters. Remove stem & strings of peas. Slice celery diagonal, 1/2". Cut green onions into 1". Thin slice red pepper. Mix soy, sherry, cornstarch, broth & 1/2 cup water; set aside. Prepare pasta & drain.

Heat 2 teaspoon oil, cook mushrooms; remove. Add 2 teaspoon oil, cook peas, celery, onions, pepper & sprouts; stir constantly, 5 minutes Stir soy mix & pour over veggies. Heat to boil.

Add pasta & mushrooms; heat through; sprinkle with peanuts.

Susan Beckman

TAGLIATELLE WITH GORGONZOLA & WALNUTS

1 # tagliatelle (long curled ball/circle pasta)
Salt & pepper
1-1/4 cups heavy cream
1 teaspoon butter
1 cup walnuts, rough chopped
1 garlic clove, crushed
1/4 # gorgonzola, crumbled

Cook tagliatelle. Drain & return to warm pan with butter, salt, pepper, and walnuts.

Make sauce: Put cream in pan, add garlic & gorgonzola & heat gently, stir occasionally, until cheese has melted. Season with salt and pepper.

Turn pasta onto large warmed dish or individual plates & pour sauce into center. Serve immediately.

LINGUINE & SHRIMP

1/2 cup Italian dressing
1/4 cup chopped parsley
1 teaspoon salt
1/2 $ shrimp
1 med, zucchini, julienned
3 green onions
1 clove garlic, minced
2 teaspoon grated lemon peel
Dash cayenne
1 med. yellow squash, julienned
1 med. carrot, julienned
1/2 # linguine, cooked

In medium skillet, heat dressing & spices. Add all other ingredients, except linguine, & saute.

Toss linguine with veggies, shrimp & sauce. Serve at once.

Susan Beckman

PASTRY

Susan Beckman

PIZZA DOUGH

2-1/4 teaspoon yeast
3-1/2 - 3-3/4 cup flour
1 teaspoon salt
2 teaspoon olive oil
1-1/4 cup warm water
1 teaspoon honey or sugar
3 teaspoon cornmeal

In stand mixer with dough hook, mix yeast & water; stir for a second. Sit 5 minutes Add 3-1/2 cup flour, honey, salt & olive oil. Mix 1 minutes on lowest setting. Knead 8-9 minutes on low-med. speed. If wet add 1 teaspoon flour at a time. Should be smooth; not sticky. Put in bowl; coat with oil; Cover with plastic wrap. Rise 1-2 hours. Punch; divide into 2; roll in ball & rest 15 minutes. Can cover with plastic & fridge; remove 30 minutes prior to using. Can also freeze in oiled Ziploc. Thaw overnight or 12 hours.

Preheat over at 480 with stone. Make pizza on parchment; let dough rest 15-20 minutes. Brush with olive oil; add sauce and toppings. Transfer to stone. Bake 10-15 minutes.

I searched for years for the perfect pizza dough recipe. Finally found it with this one. I won't use anything else for our pizza.

Susan Beckman

PIE CRUST
in stand mixer

2-1/2 cup flour
1/4 cup shortening
6-10 teaspoon water
1-1/4 teaspoon salt
10 teaspoon butter, cold & cubed

With beater attachment at 2 speed, mix flour, salt & shortening until evenly crumbly mixture. Add butter and mix until dime-size chunks of butter. Slowly add water. Stop when forms larger clumps. Squeeze handful; should hold together. Then add remaining water to come together without crumbs in bowl.

Put on parchment paper. Spray with cold water to dry/sandy parts. DO NOT SOAK. Fold parchment 1/2 over and press. Do other side. May look dry.

Divide in two. Chill 30 minutes. Or freeze.

Same with this recipe - took me years to find a good one and this is it - plus it's easy!

Farmhouse Cookbook

Susan Beckman

PIES

Susan Beckman

APPLE PIE WITH OATMEAL TOPPING

9-inch pie shell
5 cups apples, peeled & sliced
2 teaspoon flour
2 teaspoon cornstarch
2/3 cup sugar
½ teaspoon cinnamon
¼ teaspoon nutmeg
¼ teaspoon allspice
2 teaspoon butter
¾ cup flour
½ teaspoon cinnamon
½ cup brown sugar
¾ cup oats
1 teaspoon lemon zest
½ cup butter

Preheat oven to 425. Put pie shell in freezer. Mix 2 teaspoon flour, sugar, cornstarch, cinnamon, nutmeg & allspice. Mix well & add to apples. Toss until apples are evenly coated.

Place mixture into pie shell & dot with 2 teaspoon butter. Lay foil on top, but don't seal. Bake 10 minutes.

Make streusel with remaining ingredients, cutting in ½ cup butter until crumbly. Sprinkle over pie. Reduce heat to 375; Bake 30-35 minutes.

Susan Beckman

NANTUCKET CRANBERRY PIE

2 cups raw cranberries
1/2 cup sugar
1/2 cup chopped walnuts
1 cup sugar
3/4 cup melted butter
1 cup flour
1 teaspoon almond extract
2 beaten eggs

Grease 10" pie plate. Wash & pick over berries. Put on bottom of pie plate. Sprinkle with the 1/2 cup sugar & walnuts.

Make a batter of the 1 cup sugar, butter, eggs, flour & flavoring. Pour batter over berries.

Bake at 325° for 35-40 minutes. Serve with whipped cream.

FRESH FRUIT PIE

1/4 cup cornstarch
1-1/2 cups sugar
1-1/2 cups water
3 oz. Jell-O
Baked pie crust
Fruit of choice

Cook cornstarch, sugar & water until thick & clear. Add Jell-O.

Cool. Add fruit.

Pour into baked crust. Chill.

Susan Beckman

APPLE CRUMB PIE

1 pastry shell
2/3 cup flour
1/3 cup butter
1 can (21 oz) apple pie filling
1/3 cup brown sugar
1/2 cup coarsely chopped walnuts

Spoon apple pie filling in pie shell. Mix flour & sugar. Work in butter to form small clumps.

Mix in nuts. Sprinkle over pie.

Bake 35 minutes at 375.

CROSS CREEK LIME PIE
(VERY RICH)

2 cans Eagle Brand
1/3 cup lime juice (2 limes)
3 teaspoon rum
1/2 pt. cream
  (whipped with 2 teaspoon powdered
  sugar & 1 teaspoon rum)
2 grated limes
3 egg yolks, beaten
9" graham cracker crust

Add grated lime & juice to milk. Beat in egg yolks.

Add rum & food coloring. Pour into crust & top with whipped cream.

Chill until set

BANANA MALLOW PIE

2 cup coconut
3-1/2 oz instant vanilla pudding
1-1/2 cup mini marshmallows
1/3 cup melted butter
1/2 cup whipped cream
2 sliced bananas

Mix coconut & butter in skillet. Cook over low heat, stirring frequently, until coconut is toasted & brown. Press into 9" pie plate. Chill.

Prepare pudding, except use 1-3/4 cup milk. Cover & chill.

Fold in whipped cream & marshmallows into pudding. Slice bananas into crust. Pour filling over bananas.

Chill several hours.

BROWN SUGAR CHESS PIE

1 # brown sugar
4 eggs
1/4 cup milk
1-1/2 teaspoon vanilla
1/2 teaspoon salt
1/2 cup melted butter

Blend all, except butter, then mix in little at a time; pour in unbaked 9" pie shell.

Bake @ 325 for 1 hour. Cool to room temp. Cut <u>small</u> pieces.

Similar to what my mom would let us kids make with the scraps of leftover pie crust. We would mix brown sugar with a little milk, pour it in a mini pie thing, bake it, and then get bad news the next time we visited the dentist!

Susan Beckman

TURTLE PUMPKIN PIE

1/4 cup + 2 teaspoon caramel topping, divided
1 graham cracker pie crust (6 oz.)
1/2 cup + 2 teaspoon pecan pieces, divided
1 cup cold milk
2 pkg. (4-serving each) Jell-O vanilla instant pudding
1 cup canned pumpkin]
1 teaspoon ground cinnamon
1/2 teaspoon ground nutmeg
8 oz. Cool whip, thawed, divided

Pour 1/4 cup caramel topping into crust; sprinkle with 1/2 cup pecans. Beat milk, pudding mixes, pumpkin & spices with whisk until blended; Stir in 1-1/2 cup cool whip. Spread into crust. Top with remaining cool whip.

Refrigerate 1 hour. Top with pecans & drizzle remaining caramel with fork. Store leftovers in fridge.

10 servings

CARAMEL APPLE PIE

1/3 cup melted butter
1 teaspoon cinnamon
4 # apples (Fuji or Granny Smith)
  Cored & cut into 1/4-inch slices
  About 12 cups

1 recipe Oat Pastry (to follow)

1/2 cup brown sugar
2 teaspoon flour
1/2 teaspoon salt
1 egg, lightly beaten
1 teaspoon water
12 oz. caramel topping (1 cup)

Preheat oven to 475. In large bowl combine butter & cinnamon; add apples & toss gently to coat. Spread apples evenly in parchment paper or foil-lined large roasting pan. Roast 4-5 inches from heat for 7 to 10 minutes or until apples start to brown on edges, turning once halfway through. Cool apples in pan. Reduce heat to 375.

Prepare Oat Pastry or let refrigerated pastry stand at room temp. Line 9-inch pie plate with half of pastry. In very large bowl, stir together brown sugar, flour & salt. Add apple slices & any juices; stir to coat. Transfer to pastry-line pie plate.

On lightly floured surface roll remaining dough

to 14" circle; cut slits for steam to escape. Place
on top of fruit filling. Trim top crust to 1/2"
beyond edge of pie plate. Fold top pastry edge
under bottom pastry; crimp edge. Brush top with
mixture of beaten egg & water. Cover edge of
pie with foil to prevent overbrowning.

Place on middle rack; place foil-line baking sheet on
lower rack. Bake 30 minutes; remove foil from pie.
Bake for 35-40 minutes more or until top is golden
& filling is bubbly. Remove to wire rack.

While warm, drizzle with some of the caramel
topping. Cool completely. Serve with remaining
topping.

8 servings

OAT PASTRY

2 cup flour
1/2 cup quick-cooking oats
1 teaspoon salt
2/3 cup shortening
8-10 teaspoon cold water

In medium bowl stir together flour, oats & salt. Using pastry blender, cut in shortening until pieces are pea size. Sprinkle 1 teaspoon water over part of mixture; gently toss with fork.

Push moistened dough to side of bowl. Repeat, using 1 teaspoon water at a time, until all dough is moistened.

Divide in half; form each half into a ball.

Susan Beckman

PECAN PIE

9" unbaked pie shell
1 cup pecan halves
1 # brown sugar
1/4 cup flour
1/2 teaspoon salt
1/2 cup milk
1-1/2 teaspoon vanilla
3 eggs
1/2 cup melted butter

Arrange pecans in rings. Blend sugar, flour & salt; mix in milk & vanilla. Beat in eggs, one at a time; mix in butter, little at a time.

Pour over pecans.

Bake @ 325 for 1 hour 15 minutes Serve at room temp. Cut <u>small</u> pieces.

FRENCH SILK CHOCOLATE PIE

8" baked pie shell

Cream 5 minutes:
1/2 cup butter (cold)
3/4 cup super-fine sugar

Add & beat 5 minutes:
2 oz. (2 sq.) unsweetened chocolate, melted & cooled
1 teaspoon vanilla
2 eggs, cold

Cool in fridge. Put whipped cream on top & chocolate shavings.

Refrigerate.

Susan Beckman

AMISH SUGAR CREAM PIE

¾ cup white sugar
2 cup half-and-half cream
¼ cup brown sugar
½ cup butter
1/8 teaspoon salt
½ cup whipping cream
¼ cup cornstarch
1 teaspoon vanilla

In saucepan mix white sugar, salt, half-and-half & whipping cream. Bring to boil.

In another saucepan, mix brown sugar & cornstarch. Gradually whisk hot mixture into brown sugar mixture. Add butter. Cook over medium heat, whisk constantly, 5 minutes or until thick. Simmer 1 minute and stir in vanilla.

Pour into uncooked pie shell & sprinkle with cinnamon & nutmeg. Bake at 375 for 25 minutes.

This is a Midwest staple. Takes a little bit of time to make, but well worth it.

PUMPKIN PIE

9" unbaked pie shell

3/4 cup sugar
1 teaspoon cinnamon
1/2 teaspoon ground ginger
1/4 teaspoon ground cloves
2 large eggs
15 oz. pure pumpkin
12 oz. evaporated milk

Mix sugar, salt, cinnamon, ginger and cloves in small bowl. Beat eggs in large bowl. Stir in pumpkin and sugar-spice mixture. Gradually stir in milk.

Pour into pie shell.

Bake in 425 oven for 15 minutes. Reduce temperature to 350 and bake for 40-50 minutes or until knife inserted near center comes out clean. Cool on wire rack for 2 hours. Serve immediately or refrigerate.

NOTE: Do not freeze pie, as this will cause the crust to separate from the filling.

Susan Beckman

PORK

Susan Beckman

CHERRY PORK CHOPS

6 pork chops
Cherry pie filling
1/2 teaspoon chicken bouillon
2 teaspoons lemon juice
1/8 teaspoon mace (optional)

Brown chops. In crock pot, mix pie filling & remaining ingredients. Place chops on top.

Cover & cook on low 4-5 hours.

LEMON-BASIL PORK CHOPS

4 boneless pork chops
1 egg, lightly beaten
1 teaspoon lemon juice
2 teaspoons grated lemon peel
1 teaspoon dried basil
1/2 cup seasoned bread crumbs
1 tablespoon butter, melted

Mix egg & lemon juice in shallow dish. In another shallow dish, mix bread crumbs, butter, lemon peel & basil. Dip chops in egg mixture, then coat with crumb mixture.

Place in 9 x 13 x 2 baking dish coated with Pam. Bake uncovered at 375° for 30-35 minutes or until meat thermometer reads 160 & juices run clear.

JAMBALAYA

- 1/2 # fresh pork
- 1 onion, fine chop
- 1 clove garlic, fine chop
- 1/2 # ham
- 6 smoked pork sausage
- 2 teaspoon butter or lard
- 1 bay leaf – 1 sprig parsley
- 1/4 teaspoon thyme
- 1 whole clove garlic
- 1-1/2 qt. beef or chicken broth
- 1/2 teaspoon Tabasco
- 3/4 teaspoon salt
- 1 cup uncooked rice

Cut pork in 1/2" square cubes; dice ham & sausage. Melt lard in pot; add onion, garlic, pork & harm; brown slowly. Add sausage & spices. Cook 5 minutes Add broth, Tabasco & salt; bring to boil. Add rice.

Cover & simmer gently 30 minutes or longer until rice is tender.

Susan Beckman

SAUCY PORK & NOODLE BAKE

1 cup cubed cooked pork
1 teaspoon shortening
1/2 cup narrow raw noodles
1 can cream chicken soup
8 oz. corn
1 teaspoon pimento
1/2 cup cheese
1/4 cup green pepper

Brown meat. Add remaining ingredients. Pour in 1-qt. casserole dish.

Bake @ 375 for 45 minutes Stir occasionally

STIR-FRY PORK WITH BABY CORN

1 # boneless pork
2 cloves garlic
1/4 teaspoon pepper
4 teaspoon oil
1 sm. onion, 1/4" strips
1/4 # mushrooms
8 green onions, 2"
1 # baby corn

MIX & SET ASIDE:
1-1/2 teaspoon cornstarch
1 teaspoon sugar & vinegar
1/4 teaspoon salt
2 teaspoon soy
3/4 cup beef broth

Cut pork in 1-1/2" strips. Mix garlic & pepper with pork. Set aside. Put wok on high; add 1 teaspoon oil. Add 1/2 pork, cook 4 min; remove & cook other 1/2.

Heat 2 teaspoon oil. Add onion & mushrooms, 1 minutes Add green onion, 30 seconds Add pork with corn & cooking sauce. Cook 1 minute.

Susan Beckman

ROAST PORK

5 # pork roast
Garlic cloves
3-1/2 # potatoes
2 cup onions
1/3 cup parsley
1/4 cup melted butter
1 teaspoon marjoram
1 teaspoon salt
1/4 teaspoon pepper

Poke holes all over roast and stick cloves of garlic in each hole, fat side up. Roast uncovered 1 hour at 350. Mix sliced potatoes, onion & butter with spices.

Drain fat; put potatoes under roast. Roast @ 400 for 1 to 1-1/2 hours.

This is the only way I make a pork roast. And if you like garlic, you can load it up! When it cooks, the garlic gets dark and crunchy!

BBQ CURRIED PORK CHOPS

4 thick pork chops, 1-1/2 #
1 med. minced onion
1 clove minced garlic
1/4 cup each lemon juice & corn syrup
1 teaspoon oil
2-3 teaspoon curry
1/2 teaspoon salt
1/8 teaspoon pepper

Cook onion, garlic & curry in oil 2 minutes Remove from heat. Add lemon juice, syrup, salt & pepper.

Put chops in shallow bowl. Cover with marinade.

Turn occasionally for 2-3 hours.

Grill & baste.

Susan Beckman

SWEET/SOUR PORK

1/3 cup soy with 1/3 cup sugar
3/4 # pork, in cubes
Oil
1/4 cup cornstarch
1 garlic clove, minced
1 green pepper, 1" squares
1 carrot, strips
1 cup chicken broth
1/4 cup vinegar
2 teaspoon sugar
2 teaspoon soy
1-1/2 teaspoon cornstarch with 1 teaspoon water
2 pineapple rings, 3/4" cubes

Heat soy & sugar until dissolved. Pour over pork, cover & chill 4-8 hours, turning occasionally.

Heat oil; roll pork in cornstarch & let dry 5 minutes
Fry cubes 2-3 minutes.

Heat 2 teaspoon oil & stir fry 2-3 minutes garlic, green pepper & carrots.

Mix in broth, vinegar, sugar & soy; cover & simmer 2-3 minutes Add cornstarch mix, pineapple & pork & heat until thickened.

Serve with rice.

BBQ PORK CHOPS

8 pork chops
1/2 cup catsup
1 teaspoon salt
1 teaspoon celery seed
1/2 teaspoon nutmeg
1/3 cup vinegar
Water, less than 1 cup
1 bay leaf

Brown chops. Mix ingredients & pour over.

Bake @ 325 for 1-1/2 hours. Turn once.

Susan Beckman

JUDY'S PORK CHOPS

1 dry Lipton onion soup
5-6 pork chops
12 oz. peach or apricot preserves
½ cup water

Lay chops flat in dish. Mix remaining ingredients and pour over chops.

Bake at 375 for 30-40 minutes.

Another one from my friend, Judy Leisenheimer. Thanks, Jude!

Farmhouse Cookbook

Susan Beckman

POTATOES

Susan Beckman

BAKED POTATO CASSEROLE

8 med. potatoes, peeled & 1" chunks
1/2 cup sour cream
1/2 teaspoon pepper
6 slices bacon, cooked & crumbled
1 cup evaporated milk
1 teaspoon salt
2 cup shredded cheese, divided
Sliced green onions

Boil potatoes & drain. Add milk, sour cream, salt & pepper. Beat with mixer until smooth. Stir in 1-1/2 cup cheese & half of bacon. Spoon into greased 2-1/2 – 3 qt. casserole dish.

Bake at 350 for 20-25 minutes. Top with remaining 1/2 cup cheese, bacon & green onions. Bake 3 minutes or until cheese is melted.

PARSLIED POTATOES

1-1/2 pounds small new potatoes
1-1/2 tablespoons parsley
2 tablespoons butter

Cut away two narrow bands of peel from around middle of potatoes. Heat potatoes in salted water to cover to boiling and boil uncovered, just until tender, about 20-25 minutes.

Remove from heat & let stand until ready to serve. Drain well.

Heat butter in large skillet. Add potatoes & cook, shaking skillet until heated through. Sprinkle with salt, pepper & parsley.

Easy and simple, but yet good enough for company.

FROZEN POTATO CASSEROLE

2 pounds frozen hash browns
1-1/2 cups sour cream
1 cup diced onion
1/2 cup mayo
1 can cream of celery soup
1/2 cup melted butter
8 oz. sharp cheese OR 1 cup corn flakes

Thaw potatoes 30 minutes. Mix remaining ingredients, except cheese or corn flakes.

Place in 9 x 13 buttered dish. Top with cheese or corn flakes

Bake at 375° for 1 hour.

Can be put together day before without topping.

Susan Beckman

SWEET POTATO CASSEROLE

3 cups cooked mashed sweet potatoes
2 eggs
1/2 cup can milk
1 stick butter
1 cup sugar
1/2 teaspoon vanilla
1/2 teaspoon salt

Mix and pour in deep dish.

TOPPING:
1/3 cup melted butter
1/3 cup flour
1 cup brown sugar
1 cup chopped pecans

Mix & put on top of potato mixture.

Bake at 350° for 30-40 minutes.

I hate sweet potatoes, but I will eat these.

SPUDS A'la ELEGANT

4 cups instant mashed potatoes
   (according to directions)
1 beaten egg
8 ounces cream cheese
1/3 cup minced onion
Salt & pepper

Mix & bake at 350° for 45 minutes.

When my mom found this recipe, she made it for every holiday. You can make them ahead of time and have ready to pop in the oven, instead of mashing potatoes while company is waiting for dinner.

BAKED POTATO WEDGES

4 lg. baking potatoes, unpeeled
1-1/2 teaspoon kosher salt
1 teaspoon minced fresh garlic
4 teaspoon olive oil
3/4 teaspoon pepper
1 teaspoon minced fresh rosemary

Preheat oven to 400.

Scrub potatoes, cut in half lengthwise, then cut each half in thirds lengthwise; 6 long wedges from each potato. Place potatoes on sheet pain with remaining ingredients. Toss together with hands, making sure potatoes are covered with oil.

Spread potatoes in single layer with one cut-side down. Bake 30-35 minutes, turning to other cut side after 20 minutes Bake until lightly browned, crisp outside & tender inside. Sprinkle with salt & serve.

BAKED POTATO SLICES

1-1/2 # Yukon gold potatoes, peeled,
    very thinly sliced
2 teaspoon fresh thyme leaves
2 teaspoon olive oil
Salt & pepper

Mix all.

Generously brush large-rimmed baking sheet with oil & overlap potato slices just slightly.

Bake at 400 until golden brown & crisp in places, about 30 minutes

Susan Beckman

SHAKER-STYLE STEWED POTATOES

3 med. cooked boiling potatoes,
  peeled & cut into 1/2" slices
1 cup milk
2 teaspoon butter
salt & pepper

In 3-qt. pan over med/low heat, mix potatoes & milk; bring to boil. Boil gently 20-25 minutes, stir occasionally & until mixture has thickened & potatoes have absorbed all milk. (Stir gently to not break)

Stir in butter & blend. Add salt & pepper.

HASSELBACK POTATOES

4 med. baking potatoes
1 teaspoon salt
Paprika
1/4 cup butter, melted
1 teaspoon bread crumbs

Peel potatoes & place in cold water. Make slices 1/8" thick – not all the way through. Grease baking dish. Brush potato with 1-1/2 teaspoon butter & sprinkle with salt. Roast @ 450 for 40-50 minutes

Sprinkle with bread crumbs & remaining butter. Roast 5 minutes

Sprinkle with paprika down the center.

Susan Beckman

MASHED POTATO CAKES

Shape mashed potatoes into cakes or form into roll.

Wrap in wax paper; chill; slice.

Dip in flour.

Fry slowly in hot butter.

This is a great way to use up any leftover potatoes.

SLICED BAKED POTATOES

4 lg. or 8 med. potatoes
1 teaspoon salt
4 teaspoon butter

Peel potatoes. Cut thin slice off bottom. Thinly slice crosswise, but not all the way. Use wooden handle to prevent. Put on baking dish. Fan slightly. Sprinkle with salt. Add topping. Dot with butter. Bake @ 425 for 1 hour.

Cheese Topping:
4 teaspoon grated cheese
1 teaspoon Parmesan

Onion Topping:
2 teaspoon fine onion
2 teaspoon green onion or chives

Herb Topping:
4 teaspoon mixed dried herbs or
4 teaspoon fresh herbs (thyme, marjoram dill or basil)

Spicy Topping:
1-2 teaspoon paprika, curry, fennel or cumin

Susan Beckman

STUFFED BAKED POTATOES

Bake potatoes.

Preheat broiler. Cut 1/4" lengthwise slice from top; scoop flesh into bowl. Do NOT break skins.

Mash & add milk, butter & salt. Spoon into skins & brush with melted butter.

Place on greased cookie sheet & broil 3-4" from heat for 2-3 minutes

Add any:
1 cup cheese
1/2 cup blue cheese
1/4 cup onion or chives
1 cup cooked sausage meat

POTATO-CHEESE BALLS

1/2 cup grated cheese
Salt
2 cup mashed potatoes
1/2 cup bread crumbs
1 beaten egg
1 teaspoon milk

Mix cheese, salt & potatoes. Form into balls. Roll in crumbs; dip in egg with milk.

Place on baking sheet. Bake @ 450 for 15 minutes

Susan Beckman

MASHED POTATOES

Too soggy or overcooked – Sprinkle with dry powdered milk.

POTATO THING

Red potatoes, quartered
Vidalia onion, chunks
Red pepper, chunks
Garlic
Garlic salt
Stick butter

Roll in foil.

Bake 2 hours at 275.

Susan Beckman

RE-BAKED POTATOES

2 large potatoes
1/2 cup cottage cheese
1/2 teaspoon each salt & pepper
1/2 cup cheddar cheese
2 teaspoon mustard
1/2 teaspoon paprika
3 teaspoon mayo
1 egg, hard boiled, chopped
1/2 teaspoon dill weed
1/4 teaspoon cayenne
1 medium tomato
Extra cheese

DO AHEAD: Bake potatoes. When cool, slice in half laterally & scoop out insides, leaving skins intact. Place potato innards in bowl & marsh with mayo & cottage cheese. Add all remaining ingredients, except tomato, paprika & extra cheese. Mix well.

Divide filling evenly among potato skins. Slice tomato into rounds & place on top of each potato. Sprinkle extra cheese over tomatoes & dust with paprika. Place in shallow baking dish. Bake at 375 for 35 minutes.

POTATO RATATOUILLE

2 large onions, chopped
1/4 cup water
4 zucchini, sliced
4 cups (32 oz.) tomatoes, chopped
1 teaspoon oregano
2 garlic cloves, minced
3 green peppers, chopped
2 large potatoes, peeled & chopped
1 teaspoon basil
2 teaspoon parsley

Place onions & garlic in large pot with water. Cook & stir for 3 minutes.

Add remaining ingredients, except pepper. Cover & cook over medium heat for 30 minutes, stir occasionally.

Season with pepper before serving.

Susan Beckman

PRESERVES

Susan Beckman

PICKLED WATERMELON RIND

4 qt watermelon rind (white only)
2 gallons water, divided
1/2 teaspoon mustard seed
7 cup sugar
1 cup salt
3 cup white vinegar
1 teaspoon whole, assorted peppercorns
3 1-qt. canning jars

Cut rind into 1-inch cubes. In large bowl stir salt into 1 gal. Add rinds & sit overnight. Drain & rinse.

In large pan over med-high heat, cook rind with 1 gal water until tender, about 5 minutes. Drain & set aside. Heat vinegar, sugar & spices. Bring to boil, then simmer for 10 minutes. Add rinds & cook until transparent, about 10 minutes, stir occasionally.

Fill jars & process in water bath for 10 minutes.

CARAMEL SPICE PEAR BUTTER

15 pears
2 cup water
6 cup sugar
1 teaspoon ground cloves
1-1/2 teaspoon cinnamon
1/2 teaspoon ginger
2 teaspoon lemon juice

Wash & core pears. Slice into pot. Add water; cover & cook over low heat 30 minutes Let cool slightly & food process until finely chopped. Return to kettle.

In wide frying pan over med. heat, melt 1-1/2 cup sugar, stir often until carmelizes to med. brown syrup. Pour immediately into pear pulp. Stir in remaining 4-1/2 cup sugar & spices.

Bring to boil; reduce heat & cook uncovered 45 minutes until thickened. Stir in lemon juice just before removing from heat. Fills 9 1/2-pint jars. Turn upside down for 5 minutes

Farmhouse Cookbook

Susan Beckman

RICE

Susan Beckman

SPANISH RICE with BEEF

1 pound ground beef
16 oz. stewed tomatoes
1 medium onion
5 slices bacon, fried
1 cup uncooked rice
2 cups water
2/3 cup green pepper
1 teaspoon chili powder
1-1/4 teaspoon salt
1/2 teaspoon oregano
1/8 teaspoon pepper

Cook meat & onion; drain. Stir in remaining ingredients.

In skillet: Heat to boiling. Reduce heat. Cover & simmer 30 minutes.

In oven: Pour into ungreased 2-quart casserole dish. Cover & bake at 375° for 45 minutes.

Susan Beckman

GRANDMA'S RICE PUDDING

1 cup Minute rice
2 teaspoons nutmeg
4 cups milk
2 teaspoons cinnamon
1 cup white sugar

Mix all of the above & bake at 350° for 1-1/2 hours.

My mom made this usually on a Sunday afternoon in the same stainless steel bowl she made the peach cobbler.

RICE-A-RONI

1 cup white rice
2 cup chicken broth
1-1/2 teaspoon dry parsley, crushed
1/4 teaspoon salt
1/3 cup cut spaghetti
3 teaspoon butter
1/4 teaspoon granulated garlic
1/8 teaspoon pepper

Melt butter. When sizzles, add spaghetti & rice. Keep stirring until starts to brown a bit.

Turn to medium low & add dried herbs. Stir & slowly add broth.

Turn heat up so it bubbles. Put lid on, turn head down to low and cook for 15 minutes.

I just recently found this recipe. The "cut" spaghetti you can do by breaking angel hair pasta into 1/2" pieces.

Susan Beckman

SPINACH-PEA RISOTTO

2 cloves garlic, minced
2 teaspoon olive oil
1 cup Arborio rice (or short-grain)
1/2 cup thinly sliced carrots
28 oz. broth (3-1/2 cups)
Parm-Reggiano cheese
2 cup fresh spinach, coarsely chopped
1 cup frozen peas
2 oz Parm-Reggiano, shredded
1/3 cup thinly sliced green onions
1/4 cup thin wedges fresh radishes
2 teaspoon snipped fresh tarragon

In 3-qt. Saucepan cook garlic in hot oil over med. Heat for 30 seconds. Add rice. Cook about 5 minutes or until rice is golden brown, stirring frequently. Remove from heat. Stir in carrots. In 1-1/2-qt. saucepan bring broth to boiling. Reduce heat & simmer.

Carefully stir in 1 cup hot broth into rice. Cook, stirring frequently, over med. Heat until liquid is absorbed. Add 1/2 cup broth at a time, stirring frequently until broth is absorbed before adding more broth (about 22 minutes) Stir in any remaining broth. Cook & stir just until rice is tender & creamy. Stir in spinach, peas, cheese, onions, radishes & tarragon; heat through. Top with cheese shards. Serve immediately.

SLOW COOKER RISOTTO

1/2 cup wheat berries
1-1/4 # mushrooms, sliced
42 oz. broth
1-2/3 cup converted rice (no subst.)
1/2 cup chopped shallots
Italian flat-leaf parsley
3 cloves garlic, minced
1 teaspoon dried oregano, crushed
4 oz. Asiago cheese, finely shred
3 teaspoon butter, cut up
1 cup sliced fresh mushrooms
1 small yellow pepper, chopped

In small pan, mix wheat berries & 1-1/2 cup water; bring to boil. Reduce heat. Simmer, covered, 30 minutes Drain. Lightly coat inside of crock pot with Pam. Place wheat berries, mushrooms, broth, rice, shallots, garlic, oregano & 1/4 teaspoon salt & 1/4 teaspoon pepper in crock pot. Cover; cook on low 4 hours or until rice is tender

Stir cheese & butter into rice. Turn off pot; let stand, covered, 15 minutes stir in additional broth if risotto is too dry. Saute 1 cup sliced mushrooms in olive oil; set aside. To serve: Top with yellow pepper, sauteed mush, & parsley

Susan Beckman

ASPARAGUS-LEEK RISOTTO

3/4 # asparagus, trimmed
2 teaspoon olive oil
1/2 cup sliced leeks
1 cup Arborio rice
3 cup broth
2 teaspoon snipped parsley
1/2 teaspoon finely shredded lemon peel
1 teaspoon lemon juice - 1/4 teaspoon pepper
Lemon slices – lemon peel
1/3 cup grated Parmesan

Place asparagus in single layer on baking sheet. Brush with 1 teaspoon oil; lightly sprinkle salt & pepper. Bake uncovered at 450 for 10 minutes or until crisp tender. Cool slightly. Cut two-thirds in 2" pieces; set aside all asparagus.

In large pan cook leeks in remaining oil until tender. Stir in uncooked rice. Cook & stir over med heat about 5 minutes or until rice begins to turn golden brown. In another pan bring broth to boil. Reduce heat & simmer.

Carefully stir 1 cup hot broth into rice. Cook, stirring frequently, over med heat until liquid is absorbed. Add 1/2 cup broth at a time, stirring frequently until broth is absorbed before adding more (about 22 minutes) stir in remaining broth. Cook & stir just until rice is tender & creamy. Stir in asparagus pieces, cheese, parsley, lemon peel and juice & pepper. Top with asparagus spears, lemon slices & peel.

ROSY BEET RISOTTO

2 med beets
3 teaspoon olive oil
1 med red onion, chopped
1/2 cup Arborio rice (or short grain)
2 teaspoon snipped fresh basil or 1 teaspoon dried
28 oz. broth
1/2 cup crumbled blue cheese
Salt & pepper – fresh basil leaves

Heat oven to 350. Place beets in center of 18" square heavy foil. Drizzle with 1 teaspoon oil. Fold edges of foil, allowing room for steam to build. Roast 1-1/4 hours. Cool 30 minutes carefully open. Remove beets; gently transfer liquid to measuring cup; add water to equal 1/2 cup pour liquid in med pan. Cut beets in wedges.

In 3-qt. pan cook onion in oil over med heat until tender; add rice. Cook & stir 5 minutes stir in basil. Add broth to beet liquid in pan. Bring to boil. Reduce heat & simmer. Carefully stir 1 cup broth into rice. Cook stirring frequently over med heat until liquid absorbed. Add 1/2 cup broth at a time, stirring freq. until broth is absorbed before adding more (about 22 minutes)

Stir in remaining broth. Cook & stir until rice is tender & creamy. Add beets, heat through. Remove rice from heat; stir in half of cheese, basil, salt & pepper. Sprinkle with remaining cheese and basil leaves.

Susan Beckman

CUBAN FRIED RICE

1 fresh pineapple, peeled
1 teaspoon olive oil
14.8 oz. cook long-grain rice
12 oz. cook ham, coarsely chopped
1 cup chopped or sliced sweet peppers
1 jalapeno pepper, sliced
3/4 cup black beans
Lime wedges

Remove pineapple from can; reserve juice. Cut in 3/4" slices. Heat oil in skillet over med/high heat; add pineapple slices. Cook 3-4 minutes or until beginning to brown. Divide pineapple among four plates.

Prepare rice according to package. Add ham & peppers to skillet; cook 3 minutes, stirring occasionally. Add beans & rice. Cook, stirring occasionally, 2 minutes or until heated through. Stir in reserved pineapple juice. Serve with lime wedges.

BEEF BURGUNDY WITH RICE

5 med. onions, thinly sliced
2# beef chuck, cut into 1-1/2" cubes
1/2 cup beef bouillon
1/2 # fresh mushrooms, sliced
4 cups hot cooked rice
2 teaspoon bacon drippings or shortening
2 teaspoon flour
Salt, pepper, thyme, marjoram
1 cup dry red wine

In heavy skillet, cook onions in oil until brown; remove & set aside. Add more oil if necessary. Add beef cubes & brown well on all sides. Sprinkle beef with flour & seasonings. Stir in bouillon & wine. Cover & simmer very slowly for 2-1/2 to 3 hours, or until meat is tender. If necessary, add more bouillon & red wine (1 part bouillon to 2 parts wine) to keep meat barely covered with liquid.

Return onions to pan and add mushrooms. Cook 30 minutes longer, adding more liquid if necessary. Adjust seasonings to taste. Serve over hot cooked rice.

FRIED RICE

3-4 cups cooked rice
1 egg
1 clove garlic, minced
1/4 cup soy cause
1 cup peas
3 teaspoon oil
4 green onions, sliced
1/2 # shrimp or pork, etc.
1/2 cup water chestnuts

Chill rice. Heat 1 teaspoon oil at 200. Add egg & scramble; remove & set aside.

Turn to 250 & add remaining oil, onion & garlic. Stir fry 1 minute.

Stir in meat & water chestnuts. Cook 4 minutes. Stir in rice & soy sauce; then peas & egg.

This is even better than the restaurant version.

SPANISH RICE

2 teaspoon oil
1 # ground beef
1/2 cup diced onion
1/4 teaspoon pepper
2 teaspoon salt
1-1/3 cup rice
1 teaspoon Worcestershire
1 can tomatoes
1 can tomato sauce

Brown meat & onion. Add other ingredients. Cover.

Reduce to lowest heat & cook 10 minutes.

ANJU'S RICE

1 cup rice, cooked with salt & butter
2 cloves garlic
Coriander
Cashews
Salt
1/2 teaspoon cayenne
1 potato
1 onion (cut tiny)
1 green pepper
Peas
Raisins
1/4 teaspoon tumeric
Sugar

Put cooked rice on plate, spread out & cool & separate.

Saute potato, onion, garlic, green pepper, peas, cashews, raisins, & salt in oil. Mix into rice.

Add spices. Put coriander on top.

I got this from a girl I used to work with at the hospital. I think she was Indian.

NAMELESS RICE

BBQ MEAT:
2 # ground beef, browned
1 onion
1/2 cup catsup
2 teaspoon brown sugar
2 teaspoon vinegar
2 teaspoon mustard
1 teaspoon Worcestershire

CHEESE SAUCE:
2 teaspoon flour
2 teaspoon melted butter
2 cups milk
1/2 teaspoon salt
1/8 teaspoon pepper
1 cup diced cheese
Peas & cooked rice

Put rice on plate, then meat, then peas, then cheese sauce.

Susan Beckman

Farmhouse Cookbook

Susan Beckman

SALADS

Susan Beckman

BLT SALAD

8 slices bacon
2 teaspoon olive oil
1/3 cup buttermilk
2 teaspoon cider vinegar
1 pound romaine, chopped
½ baguette, ¾" cubes
Coarse salt & pepper
3 teaspoon mayo
1 scallion, thinly sliced
1 pint cherry tomatoes, halved

Preheat oven to 375. Put bacon on parchment on cookie sheet and back about 15 minutes. Cool. Crumble into large pieces.

Make croutons: Toss bread with oil, salt & pepper. Spread evenly on baking sheet. Bake until brown, tossing halfway, 15-20 minutes.

Mix buttermilk, mayo, vinegar, scallion, salt & pepper. Add lettuce, tomatoes & croutons; toss to coat with dressing. Sprinkle with bacon.

Serves 4

Susan Beckman

MOM'S MACARONI SALAD

2 pounds macaroni (cooked)
Diced sweet pickles
Hard-boiled eggs
Diced celery
Salt & pepper

Shake in jar:

1 quart mayo
1/2 cup sugar
1/2 cup sweet pickle juice
Milk to gravy thickness
Paprika

Mix all together and chill.

This is my birth mom's made-up recipe. My kids love it. It makes a lot so there's always enough left over for days to come.

BROCCOLI SALAD

1 head broccoli, cut in small pieces
1 pound bacon, fried & crumbled
1 chopped onion
1/2 cup raisins
1/2 cup sugar
1 cup mayo
2 tablespoons vinegar

Mix broccoli, onion, bacon & raisins. Can keep overnight in fridge.

Mix remaining ingredients and pour over veggie mixture.

Susan Beckman

5-CUP SALAD

1 cup mandarin oranges
1 cup seedless white grapes
1 cup pineapple tidbits
1 cup small marshmallows
1 cup sour cream
Maraschino cherries

Mix and chill.

My mom made this for every holiday. Us kids liked it because of the maraschino cherries!

LAYERED LETTUCE SALAD

1 head lettuce, broken up
6 stalks celery, chopped
1 large onion, chopped
1 # fried bacon

DRESSING:
1 cup mayo
1/2 cup sugar
1 cup sour cream
Parmesan cheese

Layer veggies in order given. Mix dressing & pour over top. Sprinkle Parmesan cheese on top.

Refrigerate for 24 hours.

ORIENTAL CHICKEN SALAD

Frozen chicken nuggets
1 cup red cabbage
3 cups romaine lettuce
1/2 carrot, shredded
1 cup Napa cabbage
1 green onion, chopped
1 tablespoon sliced almonds
1/3 cup chow mein noodles

DRESSING:
1/4 cup mayo
1/8 teaspoon sesame oil
1-1/2 tablespoon rice wine vinegar
1 teaspoon Dijon mustard
3 tablespoons honey

Cook chicken nuggets as per instructions. Toss chopped lettuce, cabbage & carrots. Sprinkle onions on top, then almonds, then chow mein noodles. Pile chicken in middle.

Serve with dressing.

I'm addicted to this salad, which is similar to a popular restaurant!

GEORGIA CRACKER SALAD

1 sleeve saltine crackers
1 large tomato, finely chopped
3 green onions, finely chopped
1-1/2 cups mayo
1 hard-boiled egg, finely chopped

Crush crackers. Mix all ingredients together and serve immediately.

Susan Beckman

KIDNEY BEAN SALAD

1 can kidney beans, drained
1-2 dill pickles, diced
Small onion, minced
1/4 cup mustard
4-6 eggs, boiled & diced
2-3 sweet pickles, diced
3/4 cup mayo
1T sugar
1 teaspoon vinegar
1 teaspoon milk

Mix all together.

This is another Midwest favorite.

DUTCH LETTUCE

1 heads lettuce
Med. onion, finely chopped
4 med. potatoes, boiled & pared
2 teaspoon butter
1/3 cup vinegar
1 teaspoon mustard seed
4 hard-boiled eggs
8 slices bacon
2 teaspoon cornstarch
2/3 cup water
salt & pepper

Tear lettuce in medium-sized pieces & put in lg. bowl. Sprinkle onion on top. Cut eggs into 1/8's & put on top. Fry bacon; drain; crumble on top. Cut potatoes in 1/2" cubes & fry.

Melt butter; add cornstarch, vinegar & water; cook, stir often, until thick & clear. Put potatoes on top with bacon fat. Sprinkle mustard seeds, salt & pepper. Pour hot sauce over all & toss.

Serve at once.

MIXED VEGIE SALAD

24 oz. frozen mixed veggies
1/4 cup scallions, chopped
1/4 cup green pepper, chopped
1/2 cup mayo
1/4 cup Fresca
salt & pepper

Mix mayo with Fresca; set aside. Cook veggies. Add scallions & green pepper & cool.

Add dressing and salt & pepper. Chill. Garnish with tomato wedges.

HARDTACK SALAD

1/2 cup red wine vinegar
salt & pepper
1/2 cup water
3 hardtack biscuits OR
   3 cups stale Italian bread in bite-sized pieces
2 cloves garlic
1-1/2 teaspoon basil
1 cup olive oil
6 tomatoes, wedged
3 small onions, ringed
6 pepperoncini

Soak hardtack in 1/2 of dressing for 30 minutes
Top with tomatoes, onions, and pepperoncini.

Pour remaining dressing on top & toss.

I've read that this recipe originated back in the Western days. As people traveled in their covered wagons across the country their bread would be stale and hard. This was their way of being frugal.

Susan Beckman

GOLDEN POTATO SALAD

4 cup cooked diced potatoes
4 hard-boiled eggs, chopped
1 cup chopped green/red pepper

1/2 cup chopped pickle or relish
1/2 cup sliced green olives
1 med. red onion, diced

Mix & add dressing. Let chill 2-3 hours.

DRESSING:
9 oz. mild cheddar cheese dip
1/2 cup sour cream
2 teaspoon mustard
3/4 teaspoon salt
2 teaspoon celery salt
Pepper

SPINACH SALAD

2 # spinach
2 cup water chestnuts
1 cup bean sprouts
1 large onion, rings
4 hard-boiled eggs, chopped
1/2 # bacon, fried

DRESSING mix in blender:
1 cup oil
1/2 cup vinegar
3/4 cup sugar
2 teaspoon salt
1/3 cup catsup

Mix ingredients., except bacon. Toss with dressing & sprinkle with bacon.

Susan Beckman

COCA-COLA SALAD

3 oz. cherry Jell-O
3 oz. strawberry Jell-O
16 oz. dark bing cherries
8 oz. cream cheese
12 oz. Coke
1 cup chopped pecans
20 oz. crushed pineapple

Drain cherries & pineapple; reserve juice & heat & dissolve Jell-O. Cut cream cheese in very small chunks & add to Jell-O. Add cherries, pineapple, Coke & pecans.

Pour into mold & chill.

JULIET'S RIBBON SALAD

3 oz. orange Jell-O
1-1/2 cup strawberries
1 envelope unflavored Jell-O
1/2 cup cold water
1 cup mayo
3 oz. cream cheese
3 oz. lemon Jell-O
1-1/2 cup blueberries

Prepare orange Jell-O using 1-3/4 cup water; add strawberries. Chill. Soften unflavored Jell-O in cold water; stir over low heat until dissolved. Gradually add mayo to cream cheese; stir in Jell-O. Cool. Pour over orange layer. Chill.

Prepare lemon Jell-O using 1-3/4 cup water. Add blueberries. Cool. Pour over mayo layer. Chill

Susan Beckman

LIME JELL-O SALAD

3 oz. lime Jell-O
1 can crushed pineapple
1 cup pineapple juice
1 cup boiling water
6 oz. cream cheese, whipped
Nuts

Mix & add nuts. Chill

FRUITED GINGERALE SALAD

6 oz. orange Jell-O
3 oz. lemon Jell-O
2 cup boiling water
2 cup gingerale
1 cup pineapple tidbits, drain & save 3/4 cup juice
1 cup mandarin oranges, save 3/4 cup juice
1 cup strawberry halves
1 cup blueberries
2 cup diced bananas

TOPPING:
3 oz lemon Jell-O
3/4 cup sugar
1 teaspoon vanilla
1 cup sour cream

Mix juices, boil, & add Jell-O & sugar, vanilla & sour cream. Pour over chilled fruits & chill again

Dissolve Jell-Os in water; add gingerale. Cool. Add fruits; pour in 9x13 pan. Chill until set.

ORANGE TAPIOCA JELL-O

1 small orange Jell-O
2 small vanilla tapioca pudding
3 cup boiling water
1 can mandarin oranges, drained
1 small Cool whip

Pour water over Jell-O & pudding; stir until dissolved. Then add oranges & cool whip. Mix well

Can use pineapple tidbits instead of oranges.

GARDEN GREEK PASTA SALAD

4 cup cooked radiatore pasta
1 med chopped red pepper
1/4 cup Kalamata olives, halved
1/4 cup oil
1/2 teaspoon oregano
16 oz kidney beans, drained & rinsed
2 cup thin-sliced cucumber
1/2 cup red onion, sliced
1/4 cup parsley
1/4 cup lemon juice
1/4 teaspoon salt
1/2 cup feta cheese

Mix all except cheese. Cover & chill for 1 hour to blend flavors.

Top with cheese.

Susan Beckman

MIDSUMMER MACARONI SALAD

1 packages mac & cheese
1 cup chopped celery
1/2 cup pickle relish
1 cup cubed tomato
2/3 cup mayo
1/2 cup chopped onion
2 teaspoon mustard

Prepare mac & cheese; add remaining ingredients & chill

HIDDEN VALLEY RANCH TORTELLINI SALAD

9 oz cheese tortellini, cooked & cooled
1/2 cup cubed Swiss cheese
3/4 cup baby peas
2 cup Hidden Valley Ranch dressing
1 cup julienned ham
1 teaspoon parsley
2 teaspoon minced green onions

Mix & chill

Susan Beckman

PASTA & KIDNEY BEANS

2 cans kidney beans
1 can water
1# ziti or small-shell pasta, cooked
1 onion, chopped
1/3 cup olive oil

Mix together.

BLACK BEAN ORZO SALAD

Two 15-oz black beans, drained
2 med tomatoes, seeded & chopped
6 oz chopped spinach
1/4 cup parsley, chopped
2 teaspoon lime juice
Salt & pepper
2.5 oz olives, drained
1-1/2 cup cooked orzo
1/4 cup green onions, chopped
2 teaspoon olive oil
1 teaspoon cumin

Mix beans, olives, tomatoes, onions & parsley. Mix oil, juice, cumin, salt & pepper. Toss with bean mixture.

Stir in pasta. Serve on spinach.

4 servings

TORTELLINI WOODSMEN STYLE

1 box tri-colored tortellini
1-1/2 cup mushrooms, quartered
1-1/2 cup tomatoes, chopped
2 garlic cloves, minced
1/4 cup veggie broth
Bacon bits
1/2 cup onion, chopped
1/2 cup dry white wine
2 teaspoon parsley
1 teaspoon chives
1 teaspoon tarragon

Cook onion; add garlic & mushrooms & cook 2-3 minutes Pour in wine & cook, stir frequently until liquid is reduced by 2/3 or almost dry.

Add tomatoes, parsley, chives, tarragon & broth. Simmer 5 minutes& set aside. Cook tortellini & drain well.

Bring sauce back to simmer. Add bacon bits & tortellini. Toss lightly & serve immediately or chill.

MEDITERRANEAN ORZO SALAD

1 cup orzo
3 teaspoon oil
2 teaspoon chopped fresh basil
2 teaspoon orange juice
1/2 teaspoon grated orange zest
1-1/2 cup chopped cooked ham
1/4 cup sliced Kalamata olives
3 teaspoon pine nuts, toasted
2 teaspoon coarsely chopped sun-dried tomatoes
1/4 teaspoon salt
1/2 teaspoon pepper

Cook orzo according to package. Drain & cool.

Whisk oil, basil, orange juice, lemon juice, zest, salt & pepper in small bowl & set aside.

Transfer orzo to large bowl. Stir in ham, olives, pine nuts & tomatoes. Pour in dressing and toss to combine.

ITALIAN GARDEN SALAD

1 head romaine, chopped
1 small red onion, thin sliced
2 tomatoes, diced
1/2 cup Romano cheese, shredded
Caesar salad croutons
1 head leaf lettuce, chopped
1/2 cup banana peppers
6 oz. black olives, sliced
1/2 Parmesan cheese, grated

Dressing:
1/2 cup mayo
1/3 cup vinegar
2 teaspoon oil
1 teaspoon lemon juice
2 teaspoon Karo
1/4 cup Parmesan
1/2 teaspoon garlic salt
1/2 teaspoon Italian seasoning
1/2 teaspoon parsley flakes.

Mix salad in large bowl. Sprinkle with Romano & Parmesan. Top with croutons.

Whisk dressing in small bowl. Before serving, pour dressing over salad to coat.

Serves 10-15

JELL-O IN A CAN

Can sliced pineapple, drained
1 cup boiling water
3 oz. box Jell-O

Dissolve Jell-O in water. Can also use pineapple juice & water to equal 1 cup liquid.

Pour over pineapple rings in can. Chill until set.

Run hot water on sides & bottom of can to loosen. Cut bottom of can and push mold out. Cut between pineapple slices & serve.

This is easy and great to make ahead of time and take camping. My grandkids love it.

Susan Beckman

MEXICORN-BEAN SALAD

11 oz. Mexican-style corn, drained
1 cup thin-sliced celery
1 cup chopped onion
1/4 cup salsa
2 teaspoon mustard
15 oz. red kidney beans, drained
1/4 cup cider vinegar
3 teaspoon oil
3 yellow bell peppers
Radicchio leaves

Mix all but peppers & radicchio in large bowl. Chill.

Cut peppers in 1/2 lengthwise; remove & discard seeds.

Spoon salsa into peppers & serve on radicchio.

TAFFY APPLE SALAD

1 teaspoon flour
1 egg
8 oz. crushed pineapple, drained, save juice
8 oz. cool whip
1/4 cup honey
2 teaspoon cider vinegar
4 cup (1#) red Delicious apples, unpeeled
1 cup salted peanuts

Mix flour & sugar. Beat egg & add to flour & sugar. Add vinegar & juice. Cook in small pan on low heat. Stir & cook until thick. Cool.

Pour cooled dressing over apples, pineapple & peanuts. Mix in cool whip.

Sprinkle additional peanuts over top for garnish.

Susan Beckman

ICE CREAM SALAD

2 cup boiling water
2 pkg. Lemon Jell-O
1 can crushed pineapple
1 cup crushed walnuts
1 qt. vanilla ice cream

Dissolve Jell-O in water. Drain pineapple & add to Jell-O.

Fold in ice cream until dissolved. Add walnuts.

Set in fridge until firm.

GREEK SALAD

1 head lettuce
1 large onion
1 cucumber
1 green pepper
3 tomatoes
4 radishes
1 teaspoon salt
Dash pepper & garlic salt
3 teaspoon wine vinegar
1/3 cup oil
1/4 # feta cheese
10 Kalamata olives

Serves 8

Susan Beckman

CRANBERRY FROST SALAD

1 cup fresh or frozen cranberries, chopped fine in blender
1/2 cup sugar
8 oz. cream cheese
1 med. apple, chopped fine
1 cup whipping cream
2 med. oranges
1 teaspoon vanilla
1/2 cup chopped dates

Mix cranberries & sugar; stand 10 minutes Peel & section 1 orange; reserve juice. Finely chop orange; set aside. Squeeze remaining orange to make total 1/2 cup juice; beat with cream cheese & vanilla until fluffy. Stir in orange sections, cranberries, apples & dates. Whip cream until soft peaks. Fold into cream cheese.

Put in 5-cup mold, 8x4x2 loaf pan, or 8-9 individual molds. Cover with saran wrap. Freeze 3 hours or up to one month. To serve: Stand room temp 10-15 minutes to soften slightly.

AMBROSIA FREEZE SALAD

3 oz. cream cheese, softened
1/2 cup powdered sugar
1 cup sour cream
1/3 cup orange juice concentrate, thawed
11 oz. mandarin oranges, drained
1/2 cup whipping cream
1 # can fruit cocktail, drained
1/4 cup coconut, toasted

Beat together cream cheese & sugar, gradually beat in sour cream & orange juice. Whip cream; fold into cream cheese mixture. Add fruit & orange sections.

Spread into 9x9x2 pan. Freeze until firm. Let stand at room temp about 10 minutes before serving.

Serve on lettuce leaf, sprinkle with coconut.

Susan Beckman

COTTAGE CHEESE & PINEAPPLE SALAD

Large cottage cheese
20 oz. crushed pineapple, drained
3 oz. Jell-O

Mix the above

Add:

Large cool whip
Pecans

Mix

WALDORF SALAD

1 cup diced apple
1/2 cup diced celery
Nuts
1/4 cup mayo
Pineapple
Oranges

Mix.

WHITE BEAN & TOMATO SALAD

15-19 oz. can cannellini or northern beans,
     rinsed & drained
1 small red onion, chopped
1/2 cup chopped fresh herbs,
   such as parsley, basil, oregano, thyme
3 plum tomatoes (or 2 medium sized)
     diced into 1/2" pieces
Fresh salad greens for garnish

Dressing:
1-1/2 teaspoon each balsamic vinegar & olive oil
1/4 teaspoon salt
1 lg. clove garlic, minced
Pepper

This salad is best served at room temp., within 30 minutes of prep. Toss salad ingredients together in large bowl. In smaller bowl, whisk dressing until blended. Pour over salad & toss again. Let sit 10 minutes to let flavors blend. Lay a few greens on plate, top with salad & serve.

PISTACHIO NUT SALAD

20 oz. crushed pineapple w/ juice
1 lg. box instant pistachio pudding
11 oz. mandarin oranges, drained
1 cup chopped nuts
1 cup mini-marshmallows
Cool whip, small

Mix pineapple & juice to dry pudding mix until blended.

Stir in remaining ingredients.

Store in fridge overnight.

Susan Beckman

CRUNCHY PEA SALAD

10 oz. frozen peas
1 cup diced celery
1 cup chopped cauliflower
1/4 cup diced green onion
1 cup cashews
1/2 cup sour cream
1 cup Hidden Valley dressing
Garnish w/ crumbled cooked bacon

Mix all & chill.

Garnish just before serving.

CARROT-RAISIN SALAD

3 cups raw shredded carrots
1 cup raisins
1/3 cup mayo
1/4 cup milk
1 teaspoon honey
1 teaspoon lemon juice
1/4 teaspoon salt
Walnuts

Mix & chill 30 minutes.

8 servings

This is just like the ones you see on restaurant buffets - only fresher!

Susan Beckman

SAUERKRAUT SALAD

1 medium can sauerkraut
1 med. can bean sprouts, drained
1 cup onions, sliced thin
1/2 cup green peppers, sliced thin
1/2 cup chopped pimento, lg. jar
1 cup vinegar
1 cup sugar

Bring vinegar & sugar to boil (5 minutes).

Mix all other ingredients, pour vinegar & sugar over it. Mix & cool.

Store in covered container in fridge 3 hours before serving.

Another one of Grandma Fitzie's recipes.

MEXICAN SALAD

1/2 cup mayo
1 mashed avocado
1 can refried beans
Shredded lettuce
Chopped onion
1 bag nacho chips
1 pint sour cream
1/2 pkg. Taco seasoning
Garlic salt
Chopped tomato
2 cup shredded cheese

Mix mayo, sour cream & avocado. Spread beans in large cake plate. Spread sour cream on top & sprinkle with garlic salt.

Place lettuce, tomato & cheese on top in that order.

Place chips around edges standing up.

HOT MEXICAN BEEF SALAD

1# ground beef
1/4 cup chopped onion
16 oz. Kidney beans, drained
1/2 cup Catalina dressing
1/2 cup water
1 teaspoon chili powder
1 qt. Lettuce, shredded
1/2 cup sliced green onion
8 oz. (2 cup) shredded sharp cheese

Brown meat & drain. Add onion; cook until tender. Stir in beans, dressing, water & chili powder; simmer 15 minutes

Mix lettuce & green onion. Add meat mixture & 1-1/2 cup cheese; mix lightly. Top with remaining cheese.

Variety: Serve with sour cream, avocado, tortilla chips & olives.

4-6 servings

BROCCOLI COLE SLAW

6 oz. Ramen noodles, crushed
3/4 stick butter
1/4 cup slivered almonds
24 oz. broccoli slaw
1/4 cup sunflower seeds
Chopped green onions, garnish

Dressing Mix:

3/4 cup canola oil
1/4 cup brown or white sugar
1/4 cup apple cider vinegar
Cumin, curry, lemon pepper,
celery salt

Melt butter in skillet over low/med. Heat. Add crushed noodles & almonds & saute, stirring occasionally. Whisk together all dressing ingredients. In small bowl.

Place broccoli slaw in bowl & toss with noodles, almonds & seeds. Pour dressing over salad & toss to coat.

Garnish with chopped green onions.

BLACK BEAN ORZO SALAD

Two 15-oz. black beans, drained
2 med. tomatoes, seeded & chopped
6 oz. chopped spinach
1/4 cup parsley, chopped
2 teaspoon lime juice
Salt & pepper
2.5 oz. black olives, drained
1-1/2 cup cooked orzo
1/4 cup green onions, chopped
2 teaspoon olive oil
1 teaspoon cumin

Mix beans, olives, tomatoes, onions & parsley. Mix oil, juice, cumin, salt and pepper. Toss with bean mixture.

Stir in pasta. Serve on spinach

4 servings

GREEK CHICKEN SALAD

4 chicken breasts
1 teaspoon lemon juice
1 teaspoon olive oil
1 teaspoon fresh oregano
1/4 teaspoon pepper
2 cloves garlic, minced
1/3 cup creamy cuke salad dressing
Mixed salad greens
3 med. cucumbers, seeded & coarse chopped
2 med. red/yellow tomatoes, coarsely chopped
1/2 cup sliced red onion
1/2 cup feta cheese
1/4 cup Kalamata or black olives

Place chicken in bag in shallow dish. For marinade, mix lemon juice, oil, oregano, garlic & pepper. Pour over chicken. Marinate in fridge for 4-24 hours, turning occasionally.

In med. bowl, mix cucumbers, tomatoes & onion; set aside. Drain chicken & grill. Cut in bite-size pieces. Toss with cucumber mix. Serve on salad greens. Drizzle with salad dressing. Sprinkle on feta cheese & olives.

GREEN SALAD WITH ORANGES & GOAT CHEESE

Vinaigrette:
1 teaspoon champagne or white wine vinegar
Zest of 1/2 orange – 1 teaspoon orange juice
1 teaspoon Dijon
1/4 cup olive oil
Salt & pepper

8 oz. goat cheese
1 cup finely chopped toasted pecans
1 head frisee, leaves torn
1/2 head radicchio, thinly sliced
4 Belgian endive, thinly sliced
4 oranges, peeled & segmented

Preheat oven to 350. Mix vinaigrette until emulsified. Set aside.

Cut goat cheese into 1 oz. rounds. Put pecans in pan or small bowl. Roll cheese rounds in pecans, pressing lightly so they adhere; transfer to baking sheet. Bake until cheese is just soft & warm, 5-7 minutes. In lg. bowl mix lettuces. Add dressing & toss to coat. Divide among 8 salad bowls. Using metal spatula, transfer 1 goat cheese round to each salad & garnish with orange segments. Serve immediately.

I don't know what frisee lettuce is, so I just mix it up with all different kinds.

ROAST PORK SALAD WITH GINGER-PINEAPPLE DRESSING

12 oz. pork tenderloin
1/8 teaspoon salt
1/8 teaspoon pepper
2 teaspoon honey mustard
6 cup Romaine and/or spinach, torn
2 cup pineapple chunks or peaches

Dressing:
In small bowl mix:
1/4 cup mayo
1/4 cup pineapple juice or orange juice
1 teaspoon honey mustard
1 teaspoon grated fresh ginger.

Cover & chill until serving time.

Preheat oven to 425. Trim fat from pork; sprinkle with salt & pepper.

Place on rack in shallow pan & roast 20 minutes spoon mustard on pork; roast 5-10 minutes longer or until 160. Thinly slice pork.

In 4 salad bowls arrange greens, pork & fruit. Sprinkled cracked black pepper.

Stir dressing & drizzle on salads.

PIZZA PIZZAZZ SALAD

8 oz. field greens
5 oz baby lettuce
4 cup grape tomatoes
1/2 red onion, thinly sliced in rings
1/2 red pepper, bite-size strips
15 oz. cannellini beans
6 oz. pepperoni
4 oz. crumbled blue cheese
5.5 oz croutons

Herb Dressing:
1/2 cup olive oil
1/3 cup white balsamic vinegar
1/4 cup parsley
1/4 cup basil
4 garlic cloves, minced
1 teaspoon salt
1/2 teaspoon pepper.

Cover and shake.

Mix greens & lettuce. Top with tomatoes, onion, peppers, beans, pepperoni & cheese. Cover and chill up to 6 hours.

Pour dressing over, toss to coat, sprinkle with croutons, & serve.

SUNSHINE SALAD

3 oz. lemon Jell-O
8.25 oz. crushed pineapple
1 cup boiling water
1/2 cup grated carrots

Mix water & Jell-O. Add ice to thicken. Add drained pineapple & carrots.

Chill.

RAMEN NOODLE SALAD

Salad greens – mixed
Slivered almonds

Dressing:
1/4 cup sugar
1/4 cup oil
1 seasoning packet from noodles
3 teaspoon vinegar
1 package Ramen noodles
Green onions
Mandarin oranges (optional)

Break up ramen noodles & put on cookie sheet, along with almonds & bake to light brown.

Mix above ingredients & add dressing just before serving.

ROB'S COLE SLAW

1/2 cup mayo
1/3 cup sugar
1/4 cup milk
1/4 cup buttermilk
2-1/2 tablespoons lemon juice
1-1/2 tablespoons white vinegar
1/2 teaspoon salt
1/8 teaspoon pepper

8 cups finely chopped cabbage (about 1 head)
1/4 cup shredded carrot (1 medium carrot)
2 tablespoons minced onion

Be sure cabbage & carrots are chopped into very fine pieces (about the size of rice).

Mix mayo, sugar, milk, buttermilk, lemon juice, vinegar, salt & pepper in large bowl and beat until smooth.

Add cabbage, carrots and onion and mix well.

Cover & refrigerate for at least 2 hours before serving.

Serves 10-12.

My daughter's father-in-law makes the best cole slaw and actually better than the one from a famous chicken place!

Susan Beckman

SANDWICHES

Susan Beckman

OVEN GRILLED CHEESE

Butter bread. Lay buttered side down on cookie sheet.

Put cheese on bread.

Butter other bread & place buttered side up.

Bake at 425 for 6-8 minutes.

Flip over & bake 3-4 minutes.

BEST DARN HAM SANDWICHES

2 12-oz packs Hawaiian rolls (small)
12 slices swiss cheese
2 teaspoon Worcestershire
1 teaspoon onion powder
1-1/2 # ham (NOT honey ham)
1 stick butter
1 teaspoon garlic powder
1 teaspoon poppy seeds

Two 9x13 foil pans. Place bottoms of rolls in each pan. Place ham on rolls. Place cheese on top. Put dinner roll tops on.

In pan, melt butter & remaining ingredients. Brush over sandwiches. Cover with foil & let sit in fridge for 1 hour or overnight (or bake right away).

Bake at 375 for 10 minutes with foil on; then 5 minutes or more with foil off, until cheese is melted.

Can also use turkey.

SANDWICH SPREAD

1 cup leftover meat, ground
2-4 tablespoons pickle relish
1-2 tablespoons chopped onion
Mayo

Mix all together.

Excellent way to use up leftover meat.

Susan Beckman

HAM SANDWICH

Ham
Swiss cheese
Mustard
Melted butter
Sesame seeds
Hamburger buns

Place ham & cheese on buns. Put mustard on top bun & close.

Brush with melted butter over all. Sprinkle with sesame seeds. Wrap in foil.

Bake at 300° for 30 minutes.

I was in high school the first time I had these with some people I babysat for and they had me stay for dinner. I knew I would use this recipe through my life. Great to make ahead and pop in the oven.

A&W BBQ BEEF SANDWICHES

4 cups shredded, cooked roast beef
1 cup ketchup
1 cup apple butter
1 cup Catalina dressing
1/4 cup Heinz 57 sauce
2 tablespoons Worcestershire

Combine all ingredients in 2-1/2 quart baking dish. Cover tightly & bake at 375° for 45 minutes or until piping hot.

Fill 8 hamburger buns & serve at once

Susan Beckman

CROCK POT SLOPPY JOES

3 pounds ground beef
1-2 onions, finely chopped
1 green pepper, chopped
16 oz. tomato sauce
1 cup water
2 packages sloppy joe mix

Brown meat in skillet. Put in strainer & rinse. Put in crock pot & add remaining ingredients.

Cover & cook: 8-10 hours on low 3-4 hours on high

SUSAN'S TOFU SANDWICH SPREAD

1 package tofu
5 carrots, shredded
2 stalks celery, diced
4-5 green onions, diced
1 cup mayo
2-3 tablespoon dill weed
1 teaspoon salt
6-8 drops Tabasco
4-5 tablespoon pickle relish

Mix all together. Chill. Spread on bread and enjoy!

I made this recipe up when we were vegetarians. I never told my kids there was tofu in it. I'd have to throw away the wrapper outside in the garbage can so they wouldn't see it.

HOMEMADE FROM SCRATCH SLOPPY JOES

1-1/2 # ground beef
1 small onion, finely diced
14.5 oz. diced tomatoes
1/2 cup brown sugar
1 teaspoon lemon juice
1 teaspoon Worcestershire
1 cup bacon, cooked/chopped
3 cloves garlic, minced
1 cup ketchup
2 teaspoon mustard
1 teaspoon chili powder
1 teaspoon cumin
1/4 teaspoon salt & pepper

Cook beef & onion until cooked through. Put in crock pot & mix remaining ingredients.

Cover & cook on low 5-6 hours.

Remember Manwich? We used to eat it all the time, but now I use this recipe. I make a bunch and freeze it.

FRANKENBURGERS

1 # ground beef
3 teaspoon steak sauce
1 egg
1/2 teaspoon salt
1 small onion, minced
1 cup shredded cheese
6 slices bacon, partially cooked & drained
6 hot dog rolls, toasted

Mix beef, sauce, egg, salt, onion & cheese.

Shape 6 portions in long roll. Wrap with bacon, broil. Turn carefully.

BAKED PIZZA SANDWICH

1 # ground beef
15 oz. tom. Pizza sauce
1 teaspoon oregano
2 cup Bisquick
1/4 cup Parmesan
1 egg
2/3 cup milk
8 oz. American or mozzarella slices
2 oz. mushrooms

Heat oven to 400. Cook meat & drain. Stir half tomato sauce & oregano; heat to boil. Reduce & simmer 10 minutes Mix Bisquick, egg & milk. Measure 3/4 cup batter & set aside.

Spread remaining batter in greased pan, 9x9x2. Pour remaining tomato sauce over batter, spread evenly. Layer 4 slices cheese, meat, mushrooms & remaining cheese slices on batter. Spoon rest of batter on top. Sprinkle with Parmesan.

Bake uncovered 20-25 minutes Cool 5 minutes

ROASTED PEPPERS & ALMONDS ON SOURDOUGH

1 lg. red pepper
1 lg. yellow pepper
1 lg. green pepper
1 small clove garlic, finely chopped
1/2 teaspoon pepper
1/4 teaspoon salt
1/2 cup sliced almonds
2 teaspoon olive oil
1 teaspoon balsamic vinegar
8 slices sourdough
1/4 cup thin-sliced red onion
4 leaves Romaine

Heat oven to 375. Grease baking sheet. Roast peppers, turn several times, 25-30 minutes, until skins wrinkle & blacken in spots. Place in paper bag, close & set aside 20 minutes   Clean baking sheet. Roast almonds 7-10 minutes; set aside.

Mix oil, vinegar, salt & pepper. Skin, core & seed peppers. Cut in 1" strips & marinade 15 minutes or overnight. Spread dressing on bread, then almonds, peppers, onions & Romaine.

Honey/Mustard:
1/4 cup honey
2 teaspoon Dijon mustard

MONTE CRISTO SANDWICH

1 egg
1/4 cup milk
1 teaspoon Parmesan
1 oz. ham & swiss cheese
2 slices bread
1 teaspoon butter

Mix egg, milk, Parmesan. cheese & pepper. Place ham & cheese on bread.

Dip into egg mixture, turning several times.

Heat butter in skillet. Add sandwich & cook over low heat until brown & crisp on both sides.

PANINI AVOCADO BACON SANDWICH

4 slices rustic white or wheat bread
8 slices crispy cooked bacon
1 lime
4 teaspoon olive oil
2 ripe medium avocados, mashed
Coarse salt

Drizzle oil over bread and grill until toasted, about 2 minutes.

Mix lime juice & salt with mashed avocado.

Spread avocado over both slices of bread. Top with bacon.

Susan Beckman

SAUCES

Susan Beckman

TARTAR SAUCE

1 cup mayo
1 tablespoon minced green olives
1 tablespoon sweet pickle relish
1 tablespoon minced parsley
1 tablespoon minced scallion
1 teaspoon Dijon mustard

Mix all ingredients & let stand at room temperature 10-15 minutes.

Serve with any seafood.

Susan Beckman

PESTO

Basil and/or parsley
Garlic
Olive oil
Melted butter
Salt & pepper
Parmesan cheese
Feta cheese
Walnuts and/or pine nuts

Mix in food processor.

Sorry I don't have measurements for this. I just use however much I feel like until it gets to the texture and taste that we like.

MAPLE SYRUP

2 cups water
4 cups brown sugar
2 teaspoon maple flavoring OR
1 teaspoon butter flavoring

Bring water to rapid boil. Pour in all brown sugar at once & stir until dissolved. Remove & stir in maple or butter flavoring.

Let stand 24 hours at room temperature before using.

Can be kept in fridge for 6 months.

Ever run out of pancake syrup for your kids? I did and this is a quick substitute and they might not even know!

Susan Beckman

HONEY BUTTER

1 cup honey
1/2 cup softened butter

Mix together. Serve on hot biscuits, bread, waffles or pancakes.

PIZZA SAUCE

28 oz. crushed tomatoes
1 teaspoon sugar
1/4 teaspoon oregano
2 teaspoon garlic salt
2 teaspoon dried basil
1/2 teaspoon onion powder
1 teaspoon paprika
1/2 teaspoon pepper

Pour tomatoes in bowl. Add seasonings & stir to combine.

Equals 2 jars pizza sauce.

Freezes well.

I never seemed to have those cans of pizza sauce on hand when I needed it. And it always seemed to be bland. But now I make a bunch of this and have in the freezer, ready to use.

Susan Beckman

SEAFOOD COCKTAIL SAUCE

3/4 cup chili sauce or catsup
1 teaspoon lemon juice
1/8 teaspoon pepper
Dash cayenne
2 teaspoon horseradish
1/2 teaspoon salt
1/2 teaspoon Worcestershire
Honey, to taste

Mix & chill well.

Another one of my made-up recipes. We won't use any other sauce with our shrimp cocktail.

TINA'S SWEET/SOUR SAUCE

20 oz. Crushed pineapple in syrup
1 cup water
1 teaspoon soy sauce
1 cup plum jam
1 cup sugar
1 cup vinegar
2 teaspoon cornstarch with 2 teaspoon cold water

In pan, heat all except jam. Boil 1 minutes, stir constantly.

Take off heat, cool, and then stir in jam.

GORGONZOLA SAUCE

4 cup heavy cream
3 teaspoon grated Parmesan
3/4 teaspoon pepper
3-4 oz. crumbly Gorgonzola
3/4 teaspoon kosher salt
3 teaspoon minced fresh parsley

Bring cream to full boil in medium saucepan over medium-high heat, then continue to boil rapidly for 45-50 min, until thickened like a white sauce, stirring occasionally.

Off the heat, add Gorgonzola, Parmesan, salt, pepper & parsley. Whisk rapidly until cheeses melt & serve warm.

If you must reheat, warm sauce over low heat until melted, then whisk vigorously until sauce comes together.

Barefoot Contessa

RED EYE GRAVY

1 cup strong coffee
1 teaspoon cornstarch with 2 teaspoon heavy cream

Mix with drippings from ham.

Did you know coffee was in Red Eye Gravy? Neither did I until I found this recipe.

Susan Beckman

BBQ SAUCE

1/4 cup butter or oil
1/2 cup onion
1 clove crushed garlic
12 oz. tomatoes
6 oz. tomato paste
1 teaspoon salt
1 teaspoon dry mustard
1-1/2 teaspoon Worcestershire
1 cup water
1/4 cup vinegar
1/2 cup catsup
1/4 cup molasses
1 teaspoon chili powder
1/4 teaspoon pepper
1 bay leaf
3 drops Tabasco

Heat butter. Add onion & garlic; saute 5 minutes
Stir in remaining ingredients. Bring to boil.

Reduce heat & simmer uncovered for 30 minutes
Stir occasionally.

Strain.

HORSIE SAUCE

1 cup white sauce
1/3 cup horseradish
1/4 teaspoon dry mustard
Dash paprika

Mix all together.

TINA'S TACO SAUCE

3 cups tomatoes
3/4 cups onions
3 cups or less jalapenos with seeds
1-1/2 teaspoon salt
1-1/2 cup vinegar
3 cloves garlic or more
Green peppers

Mix & bring to a boil. With lid on, simmer 5 minutes.

Pack in jars, divide all liquid evenly.

Pints = 30 minutes
Quarts = 45 minutes

SAUNDER'S HOT FUDGE SUNDAE TOPPING

12 oz. chocolate chips
14 oz. Eagle brand milk
1/2 # butter
1-2/3 cups (14 oz.) light corn syrup

In top of double boiler over simmering water, melt the above until smooth, stirring often.

Cook without stirring 30 minutes over hot water.

Put through blender until smooth.

Makes 1 quart

Susan Beckman

SOUPS

Susan Beckman

BROCCOLI & CHEESE SOUP

1 teaspoon melted butter
½ medium chopped onion
¼ cup melted butter
¼ cup flour
2 cups half-and-half cream
2 cups chicken stock
½ pound fresh broccoli
1 cup carrot, julienned
¼ teaspoon nutmeg
8 oz. grated sharp cheese

Saute onion in butter & set aside.

Cook butter & flour with whisk over medium for 3-5 minutes. Stir constantly & add half-and-half. Add chicken stock. Simmer 20 minutes.

Add broccoli, carrots & onions. Cook over low 20-25 minutes.

Add cheese & nutmeg.

Just as good as the one from that famous bread restaurant!

TERESA DALLAS' VEGIE SOUP

Roast
1 can carrots, cut in 1/4's
Large can crushed tomatoes
1 tablespoon sugar
1 can diced potatoes
1 can seasoned cabbage

Put roast in crock pot with either beef broth or water.

When done cooking, tear up & add remaining ingredients.

Can you tell by the name of the recipe who gave me this one? Yep, my long-time Air Force friend.

FREE SOUP

Leftovers (bones, meat, juices, broth, gravy)
Tomatoes
Bouillon cubes
Vegies, rice, pasta
Bay leaf, basil, thyme, parsley
Uncooked ground beef
Onion & celery
Frozen vegies

Mix all together and cook.

This is a great way to clean out the fridge!

Susan Beckman

SUSAN'S SOUP

2 zucchini
4 beets
4 carrots
2 celery
Parsley
Kale
1 large can tomato juice
2 cups water
Salt

Chop veggies. Mix all together. Heat & eat.

I made this up when we were vegetarians. And even make it now.

KANDY'S VEGETABLE SOUP

5 large potatoes   3 carrots
Lima beans
1 medium onion
2 stalks celery
5 lettuce leaves
1 cup corn
2 tomatoes
2 medium turnips
1 cup peas
3 tablespoons butter
1 tablespoon salt
1/3 cup alphabet macaroni
4 cups tomato juice
2 cups water
1/4 teaspoon pepper

Peel potato & cut into pieces; boil. Drain & save water. Slice onion & celery; set aside. Prepare other veggies.

Press potato through sieve and/or cut into chunks. Melt butter. Saute celery & onion; cook 10 minutes. Add flour. Add remaining ingredients. Cook until ready to eat.

My first granddaughter ended up in the hospital when she was 3 days old and nearly didn't make it. My daughter & I stayed the entire 10 days. My friend, Kandy Thorsen, brought us this soup and it was such comfort food at a traumatic time in our life. Every time I make this I think of how God answered our prayers for Brittney.

CREAM OF MUSHROOM SOUP

3 teaspoon butter

1/2 cup minced crimini mushrooms

1/2 cup veggie broth

Pinch salt

1 small shallot, minced

2-1/2 teaspoon flour

1/2 cup whole milk

2 pinches pepper

In skillet, melt butter over med. heat. Add shallot, stir to coat & saute 3-5 minutes. Add mushrooms, stir & cook 2-3 minutes.

Sprinkle with flour & cook for 1-2 minutes. Whisk in milk & broth until smooth. Bring to simmer & cook until thickened (5-8 minutes). Use in place of canned cream of mushroom soup. Freeze.

CREAM OF CHICKEN: Saute shallot & 1 clove garlic. Cook as above. Whisk in 1/2 cup milk & 1/2 cup chicken broth. Finish as above.

CREAM OF CELERY: Saute shallot & 1-2 ribs of celery (minced) & 1 clove garlic. Cook as above. Add 1/2 cup milk & 1/2 cup veggie broth. Finish as above

CREAM OF CHICKEN: Saute shallot & 1 clove garlic. Cook as above. Whisk in 1/2 cup milk & 1/2 cup chicken broth. Finish as above.

BAKED POTATO SOUP

6 lg. Potatoes, peeled & cut into 1/2" cubes
1 large onion, chopped
3 (14-oz.) cans chicken broth with roasted garlic
1/4 cup butter
2-1/2 teaspoon salt

1 cup whipping cream or half & half
1 cup (4 oz.) shredded sharp cheese
3 teaspoon chopped fresh chives
8 oz. sour cream (optional)
4 bacon slices, cooked & crumbled
Shredded cheese
1-1/4 teaspoon pepper

Combine potatoes, onion, broth, butter, salt & pepper in crock pot. Cover & cook on high 4 hours or low 8 hours, or until potatoes are tender.

Mash mixture until potatoes are coarsely chopped & soup is slightly thickened; stir in cream, cheese & chives. Top with sour cream, if desired, & sprinkle with bacon and cheese before serving.

Susan Beckman

CREOLE SOUP POT

6 slices bacon, 1/2" pieces
1 teaspoon minced garlic
14.5 oz. stewed tomatoes
1 bay leaf
1 # shrimp, shelled & deveined
3/4 cup green pepper, 1/2"
Two 10-oz. chicken with rice soup
1-1/2 cup water
Hot pepper sauce to taste
1/2 cup green onions

In 4-qt. pot, cook bacon until crisp; remove & drain fat to 2 teaspoon Add green onions, green pepper & garlic; cook over med. until crisp tender.

Stir in soup, tomatoes, water, bay leaf & hot pepper sauce. Bring just to boil. Reduce heat, simmer uncovered 10 minutes

Add shrimp & bacon; cover & simmer 5 minutes Discard bay leaf.

AUTUMN SOUP

1/2 # ground beef
1/2 cup onions
2 cups hot water
3/4 cup celery
3/4 cup cubed potatoes
1 teaspoon salt
1/4 teaspoon pepper
1/2 bay leaf, crumbled
Basil
3 tomatoes

Brown beef. Add onions & cook 5 minutes. Add remaining ingredients, except tomatoes & mix, loosening crust on bottom.

Boil. Cover. Simmer 20 minutes.

Add tomatoes & more water, if necessary. Simmer 10 minutes.

Susan Beckman

HOT & SOUR SOUP

Two 13-3/4 oz. chicken broth
42 oz. chicken chow mein
1/4 cup vinegar
1 teaspoon soy sauce
2 teaspoon sesame oil
1 teaspoon hot pepper sauce
1/2 teaspoon sugar
1/4 teaspoon pepper
2 green onions, slivered

Mix all, except onions & chow mein. Boil.

Drain & rinse chow mean. Add to soup.

Garnish with green onions.

VICHYSSOISE

1 teaspoon butter
4 small potatoes, peeled & cubed
1/2 teaspoon salt
1/8 teaspoon pepper
1 medium chopped onion
10 oz. chicken broth
1/2 cup water
1-1/2 cups half & half

Saute onion in butter. Add potatoes, broth, water, salt and pepper. Simmer covered about 15 minutes.

Pour in blender & add half-and-half. Blend 20-30 seconds

Susan Beckman

HAMBURGER SOUP

2 # ground beef
1 # carrots
4 medium-large onions
1 bunch celery
5-6 medium potatoes
2 cans tomatoes

Grind or chop all veggies. Brown beef; add veggies.

Cover with water. Add tomatoes.

Season with salt and pepper.

BEAN SOUP

1 # great northern beans
5 cups water
2 med. potatoes, pared & cubed
1 lg. carrot, pared & diced
1 med. onion, chopped
2 stalks celery, sliced
9 cups chicken or turkey broth
1 bay leaf
4 allspice
2 teaspoon salt
1/4 teaspoon pepper
2 teaspoon parsley

Place beans in kettle with water; bring to boil. Cover & remove from heat, let stand 1 hour.

Add potatoes, carrots, onion, celery, broth, bay leaf & allspice to beans & bean liquid. Bring to boil; lower heat. Cover & simmer until beans are tender.

Add salt, pepper & parsley.

Susan Beckman

FASS

Ham
Whole pepper corns
Milk or half-&-half
Onions
Sauerkraut juice (6-8 cans)
Spätzle

Boil ham, onions and whole pepper.

Take out ham. Add sauerkraut juice.

Cook; then cool.

Add milk or half-&-half. Add spätzle.

My friend, Judy Leisenheimer, is Polish and this is a Polish soup. The ingredients don't sound good together, but it is great. Except now I have a hard time find sauerkraut juice!

AUTUMN CHOWDER

6 slices bacon, chopped
1 cup chopped onion
1 cup water
2-1/2 cups potatoes, pared & diced
2 teaspoon chicken bouillon
3 teaspoon flour
3 cups milk
1 can each (16 oz. each) whole corn and carrots, drained
3 cups (12 oz.) shredded cheddar cheese
1/8 teaspoon white pepper

Partially cook bacon in kettle. Stir in onions. Cook until bacon is crisp. Stir in water, potatoes, carrots & bouillon. Heat to boiling; reduce heat & cover. Simmer until potatoes are tender, 15-20 minutes.

Stir in milk, corn & pepper. Heat to simmering. Mix cheese & flour; add to soup mixture, stirring constantly until cheese is melted.

CUBAN BLACK BEAN SOUP

2 # dried black beans
4 medium onions, diced
3 cloves garlic
1/2 cup tomato paste
1 bay leaf
Salt
8 oz. bacon, diced
1 red & 1 green pepper, diced
10 cups water or chicken broth
1 teaspoon oregano
1/2 teaspoon pepper
1 teaspoon lime juice

Rinse & soak beans overnight OR cover with water, boil 2 minutes, cover and stand 1 hour. Cook bacon until crisp. Add onions, peppers & garlic. Cook 5 minutes. Drain beans & add with remaining ingredients. Stir. Bring to boil. Reduce heat & simmer uncovered until beans are tender, 1-1/2 to 2 hours.

Puree 4 cups soup & stir back in. Serve with chorizo, green onions & sour cream.

8 servings

BEEF, BARLEY & KALE SOUP

1 teaspoon oil
1 # beef, 1/2" cubes
2/3 cup onion, chopped
6 cups beef broth
2 cups carrots, diced
1 teaspoon thyme
1/2 cup raw barley
1/2 teaspoon salt
10 oz. kale or 1 # fresh, steamed & chopped
8 oz. mushrooms, sliced

Heat oil. Add beef & onions & cook 4 minutes until meat is brown. Add broth, carrots, barley, thyme & salt. Bring to boil. Reduce heat. Cover & simmer 1 hour or until meat & barley are nearly tender.

Add kale & mushrooms, return to boil. Reduce heat. Cover & simmer 5-10 minutes until meat, barley & veggies are tender.

6-8 servings

Susan Beckman

GREEK LEMON SOUP

4 cups chicken broth
1/3 cup orzo
3/4 # chicken breasts
2 eggs
1 teaspoon dill
1 teaspoon parsley

Add orzo to boiling broth. Cook. Add chicken. Cook.

Mix eggs with lemon juice. Whisk in some hot broth. Add to soup. Cook.

Add dill & parsley.

GOLDEN BROTH

1 onion, chopped
1 clove garlic
1/2 cup yellow split peas
2 teaspoon oil
1/2 teaspoon tumeric
2 quarts hot water

Saute onion, whole garlic clove & peas in oil until delicately brown. Stir in tumeric & add water.

Simmer at least 1/2 hour. Strain for thin stock. Puree for thick stock.

Believe it or not, this could be a substitute for chicken broth. Nobody would know the difference unless you tell them!

Susan Beckman

FRENCH ONION SOUP

2 teaspoon butter
2 teaspoon oil
6-7 cups thinly sliced onions
1/2 teaspoon sugar
Toasted bread
1 teaspoon salt & pepper
2 teaspoon flour
Five 10-oz. beef bouillon
3 soup cans water
Grated cheese

Heat butter & oil. Add onions & sugar. Cook over medium heat for 20-30 minutes, stirring frequently until onions are lightly browned & bottom of pan is glazed.

Scrape glaze & blend with onions. Stir in flour & cook 1 minute. Stir in bouillon, water, salt & pepper. Reduce heat & simmer covered 30 minutes.

Ladle over rounds of toasted bread. Top with grated cheese.

TINA'S BROCCOLI SOUP

2 pkgs. Frozen cut broccoli
2 sticks butter
Flour
Milk
Chicken bouillon cube
Salt & white pepper
Dried onion

Melt butter. Add flour with whisk until real thick. Add milk to thin. Cook until thick. Add more milk. Add dried onion, salt, pepper, & bouillon. Simmer until thick again. Add more milk & thawed broccoli. Cook until thick.

Stir frequently. Add more milk to desired consistency.

Can add cheese on top of each bowl.

Susan Beckman

COUNTRY CORN CHOWDER

6 cups water
6 potatoes, peeled & cubed
1 medium onion, chopped
2 garlic
1/2 teaspoon salt
3-4 cups corn
2 vegie bouillon
1/4 cup minced green pepper
1/4 cup heavy cream
1/8 teaspoon sage
1/2 teaspoon thyme
1/2 teaspoon oregano
1 stalk celery, chopped
1 teaspoon butter
1 teaspoon dill
1/2 cup minced scallions

Bring water to boil; add veggies. Return to boil; add seasonings. Cover & simmer 15-20 minutes. Cool slightly. Remove 2 cups potatoes & set aside. Blend remaining chowder. Reheat over low heat, add corn & potatoes. Simmer 5 minutes.

Melt butter in skillet; add green pepper & scallions. Saute 3 minutes. Stir into chowder. Add cream & dill.

Farmhouse Cookbook

Susan Beckman

STEWS

Susan Beckman

EMMA LOU'S STEW OVER RICE

Stew meat, cut in chunks
Tomatoes, canned
Cooked rice

Brown stew meat. Add tomatoes with sauce. Cook awhile.

Serve over rice.

Back in the 1970s when money was tight, my cousin, Emma Lou, taught me how to make this frugal dish. We still make it to this day.

Susan Beckman

OVEN STEW

2 pounds beef, 2" cubes
1/4 cup bread crumbs
1 onion, quartered
2 cups mushrooms
4 carrots, halved
1 teaspoon salt
4 celery stalks, quartered
1/4 teaspoon pepper
3/4 cup wine
12 oz. tomatoes, undrained

Mix all ingredients in large kettle. Cook at 300-350° for 4 hours, covered.

DO NOT UNCOVER.

CINCINNATI CHILI

4 small chopped onions
4 tablespoons vinegar
2 # ground round
2 teaspoon cinnamon
1 small garlic clove
2-1/2 teaspoons salt
6 oz. tomato paste
2 tablespoons chili powder

PUT IN CHEESECLOTH BAG:
20 allspice balls
6 broken bay leaves, small
1 teaspoon crushed red pepper

Brown onions, beef & garlic. Add vinegar, cinnamon, salt, paste & chili powder. Tie bag & place in chili. Add 4 cups water. Cook 4 hours. Stir often. Add a little water to keep proper consistency. Take out spice bag.

Serve over spaghetti or add 1 can beans. Grated cheese and/or oyster crackers over top.

DO NOT DOUBLE RECIPE IN SAME KETTLE.

My friend, Mary Eha, gave me this recipe. My family loves it. It's similar to Skyline Chili in Cincinnati, Ohio.

Susan Beckman

FRENCH OVEN STEW

2-1/2 pounds beef stew
1/4 teaspoon pepper
4 large carrots, quartered
12 oz. small white onions
3 celery stalks, cut 1" pieces
6 oz. mushrooms
1/2 cup dry red wine or water
1 teaspoon basil
1-1/2 cups tomato juice
1 tablespoon sugar
1/2 cup quick-cooking tapioca
2 small bay leaves
2 teaspoon salt

Mix all ingredients in 3-quart ovenproof pot. Cover & bake for 3 hours at 300°, stirring three times, or until meat is tender & sauce is thickened. Discard bay leaves.

Stew begins to thicken during the last hour of cooking. The tapioca does it; if you like, add a cup of frozen green peas or cut green beans 20 minutes before stew is done.

WENDY'S CHILI

4# ground beef
3 small cans diced tomatoes
Peppers: red, yellow, green, orange
Garlic salt, basil, sugar
3 large tomato sauce
4 small cans dark red beans
Onions & garlic
Worcestershire, salt & pepper

Flatten meat in pan; drizzle with Worcestershire. Cook, Cut in quarters & flip. Sprinkle with sugar. Break up in big chunks. Can be kinda pink.

Add sauce & tomatoes, more sugar. Add veggies & beans. Stir gently. Add more sugar.

Cook 1-2 hours. Stir, add more sugar. Taste after 4 hours. Cook total of 6-7 hours.

I'm proud to say this is a recipe my daughter, Wendy, made up. Usually my girls come to me for recipes, but this one I had to learn from her. Thanks, Wendy Jean (also known as Spit Head or Marble Head)! She's gonna kill me for publishing this!

Susan Beckman

TOMATOES

Susan Beckman

FRIED GREEN TOMATOES

1 large egg, lightly beaten
1/2 cup flour, divided
1 teaspoon salt
Dash cayenne
3 med. green tomatoes, cut in slices
1/2 cup buttermilk
1/2 cup cornmeal
1/2 teaspoon pepper
1 teaspoon paprika
Vegetable oil   Salt

Mix egg & buttermilk; set aside. Mix 1/4 cup flour, cornmeal, 1 teaspoon salt & pepper. Dredge tomato slices in remaining 1/4 cup flour; dip in egg mixture & dredge in cornmeal mixture.

Pour oil to depth of 1/4" to 1/2" in cast-iron skillet; heat to 375. Drop tomatoes in batches into hot oil & cook 2 minutes on each side or until golden.

Drain on paper towels or rack. Sprinkle hot tomatoes with salt.

4-6 servings

Susan Beckman

MICHELLE'S TOMATO PIE

Pie crust, prebaked
1/2 # sliced swiss cheese
2 teaspoon Parmesan cheese
Pepper
Sliced tomatoes, with salt
1 teaspoon basil
2 teaspoon melted butter

Overlap swiss cheese, then tomatoes, pepper, basil, Parmesan & butter.

Bake 25 minutes at 375.

My cousin, Michelle, was from France. This is one of her great recipes.

SAUTEED TOMATOES

Tomatoes
Egg
Salt & pepper
Flour
Bread crumbs, Italian
Butter

Dip firm tomato slices(1/4"thick) into seasoned flour, then in egg, then in bread crumbs.

Sprinkle with salt & pepper.

Brown in butter 10 minutes.

Susan Beckman

VEGGIES

Susan Beckman

BEETS WITH ORANGE SAUCE

1 teaspoon butter
1/4 cup sugar or brown sugar
1 teaspoon cornstarch
3/4 cup orange juice
1/8 teaspoon salt & pepper
1 qt. diced beets, drained

Melt butter. Mix sugar & cornstarch; blend into butter.

Stir in orange juice & cook until thick, stir constantly.

Add salt, pepper & beets; heat through

Susan Beckman

COPPER PENNIES

5 cup sliced cooked carrots
1 med. onion, sliced
1 can tomato soup
1 green pepper, sliced
salt & pepper
1 teaspoon mustard
1 teaspoon Worcestershire
1/2 cup oil
1 cup sugar
3/4 cup vinegar

Drain & cool carrots. Mix all remaining ingredients. Together & bring to boil. Cool. Pour over carrots & marinate 12 hours before serving.

Serve hot or cold. Will keep in fridge 2 weeks & freezes well.

SUNSHINE CARROTS

5 med. carrots, 1"
1/4 cup orange juice
1 teaspoon sugar
1/4 teaspoon salt
2 teaspoon butter
1 teaspoon cornstarch
1/4 teaspoon ginger

Cook carrots 20 minutes Drain. Mix all, but butter & orange juice in small pan. Add juice; cook until thick. Stir in butter.

Pour over hot carrots, stir to coat evenly.

Susan Beckman

GOLDEN CARROT BAKE

3 cup (1 #) carrots, shredded
1-1/2 cup Coke
2/3 cup long-grain wild rice
1/2 teaspoon salt

   MIX above in pan & bring to boil. Reduce heat & simmer, covered 25 minutes Do not drain.

2 cup (8 oz.) shredded Cheddar
1 cup milk
2 beaten eggs
2 teaspoon dried onion
1/4 teaspoon pepper

Stir in remaining ingredients., reserving 1/2 cup cheese. Put in 1-1/2 qt. casserole dish. Bake uncovered at 350 for 1 hour. Top with remaining cheese. Return to over 2 minutes to melt cheese

FRIED CORN

6 ears corn
1/4 cup butter

1/8 teaspoon pepper
3/4 teaspoon salt
2 teaspoon sugar

Cut corn from cobs & scrape with knife to get milk from cob. Heat butter in skillet & add corn & juice.

Season with salt & pepper. Cover & simmer 5-10 minutes

Susan Beckman

BAKED STUFFED CUCUMBERS

2 cucumbers, peeled & halved
5-6 teaspoon melted butter
2 cup bread crumbs
1/4 teaspoon salt
1 teaspoon chervil
1/2 cup chopped tomatoes
3 teaspoon blanched almonds

Scoop seeds & center pulp. Coarsely chop & reserve 1/4 cup Parboil cukes 5 min; drain & put in buttered shallow pan.

Brush with melted butter. Toss crumbs with pulp, 1/4 cup melted butter & remaining ingredients., except almonds & drizzle with melted butter. Top with almonds.

Bake at 350 for 35 minutes

ROASTED GARLIC

1 medium to large head of garlic
Baguettes or Italian bread
Olive oil

Soak entire garlic baker in water for 5-10 minutes before using. Cut off top of garlic head. Brush garlic head with olive oil, salt and pepper.

Place garlic in baker, cover & place in a cold oven which should be brought up to 350; cook for 35-40 minutes.

To serve, simply remove individual cloves with a knife & spread on bread, with butter if desired.

Susan Beckman

QUICK CORN MAZATLÁN

17 oz. corn
4 oz. diced green chilies
1/4 cup chopped red pepper
3 oz. cream cheese
1/4 cup sliced green onions

Drain corn & save 2 teaspoon liquid. Mix with cream cheese in pan.

Heat & blend until smooth. Stir in remaining ingredients.

Serves 4-6

CORN FRITTERS

1-1/2 cups flour
2 teaspoon baking powder
1/2 cup milk
1-1/2 teaspoon salt
2 eggs
2 cups corn

Mix flour, salt, baking powder; add eggs, a little milk & beat until smooth. Add rest of milk. Stir in corn.

Fat at 375; drop by tablespoon.

Can add: 1 cup cheese; if too thick, add 1-2 tablespoons water.

These are even better with maple syrup!

SUCCOTASH

2 cups Corn
Butter
Salt
2 cups Lima Beans
Cream
Pepper

Cut corn from cob to make 2 cups (or use can corn). Cover cobs with water & boil gently 30 minutes.

Remove cobs & add 2 cups lima beans; cook until tender.

Add corn & cook several minutes. Drain. Add salt & pepper, butter & a little cream.

CARROTS

6 large carrots
1/4 cup butter
1/4 cup mustard
1/2 cup honey
2 teaspoon chives or parsley

Cook carrot slices. Drain.

Blend & cook other ingredients.

Cover carrots with sauce & heat.

Susan Beckman

BROCCOLI CHEESE SQUARES

3 teaspoon butter
3 eggs
1 cup flour
1 teaspoon salt
2 teaspoon onion, finely chopped
20 oz. frozen broccoli, chopped
1 cup milk
1 teaspoon baking powder
1 # shredded cheese
1 sprinkle seasoned salt

Grease 9 x 13 dish with butter or Pam. Steam broccoli, then cool & press dry. beat eggs & milk until frothy.

Mix flour, baking powder & salt and stir into egg mixture. Fold in broccoli, cheese & onion & pour into dish. Sprinkle with seasoned salt.

Bake for 35 minutes at 350 or until lightly browned. Let stand 5 minutes, then cut into bite-sized pieces.

BROCCOLI & CHEESE

2 pkgs. Frozen chopped broccoli
1 can celery soup
1 teaspoon minced onion
1 cup grated sharp cheese
1 teaspoon Worcestershire
2 beaten eggs
1 cup mayo
1/2 cup milk
Ritz crackers
Salt & pepper

Cook broccoli. Cool.

Mix all ingredients, except crackers. Put in buttered casserole dish. Crumble Ritz crackers over top & dot with butter.

Bake 45-50 minutes at 350.

Susan Beckman

VEGETABLE FRITTER BATTER

3/4 cup flour
1 teaspoon baking powder
1 teaspoon salt
3/4 cup milk
1 egg

Mix flour, baking, powder & salt. Slowly add milk & beat until smooth.

Add egg & beat well.

Dip vegies into batter and fry in oil. The batter puffs up!

This tastes just like the tempura fried veggies in restaurants.

BAKED ZUCCHINI

2 # zucchini
2 cups boiling water
1 onion, chopped fine
1 clove garlic, crushed
1/4 cup olive oil
1/2 lemon juice
3 teaspoon flour with 1/4 cup water
1/8 teaspoon each rosemary, savory, nutmeg
1 teaspoon salt 1/8 teaspoon pepper
1/4 cup Parmesan
1/4 cup parsley

TOPPING:
1-1/2 cups bread crumbs
2 teaspoon Parmesan   1/3 cup melted butter

Quarter zucchini in half lengthwise, then half crosswise. Place in saucepan with water. Cover & boil 15-20 minutes. Drain. Reserve 1 cup water.

Saute onion & garlic 8 minutes. Stir in remaining ingredients, except cheese & parsley. Heat until thickened. Stir constantly. Take off heat & mix in cheese & parsley. Put zucchini in buttered 8x8 pan. Cover with half sauce. Add remaining zucchini & sauce. Sprinkle topping over all. Bake uncovered 1 hour at 325.

Susan Beckman

BAKED SPINACH & CHEESE

15 oz. spinach
4 eggs, beaten
1 cup milk
1 cup Swiss cheese, shredded
1 cup cubed white bread
1/2 cup sliced green onions
1/4 cup Parmesan

Drain spinach; squeeze out liquid. Mix all.

Pour in 1-quart dish.

Cover & bake 25-30 minutes at 375.

BRUSSEL SPROUTS WITH WATER CHESTNUTS

2 teaspoon butter
2 teaspoon flour
3/4 cup chicken broth
1-1/2 cups sliced water chestnuts
1/4 teaspoon basil
3 # brussel sprouts
Salt & pepper

Melt butter. Add flour. Add broth. Cook until thick.

Season with salt, pepper & basil. Keep warm over simmering water.

Cook sprouts. Drain. Put in serving dish. Add chestnuts to milk mixture, pour over spouts.

PEAS IN ORANGE DILL SAUCE

1/2 cup red pepper strips
2 teaspoon butter
17 oz. can peas
2 teaspoon cornstarch
1/4 cup orange juice
1/4 teaspoon dill weed
1/4 cup sliced green onions

Cook pepper strips in butter until soft. Drain peas & save 1/4 cup liquid.

Dissolve cornstarch in liquid; add orange juice & dill. Add to pepper strips.

Cook & stir constantly until thick & clear.

Add peas & green onions. Garnish with grated orange peel.

Serves 4

STUFFED PEPPERS

6 medium green peppers
16 oz. tomatoes, coarse chopped
1/2 cup green onions, sliced
1-1/2 teaspoon coriander
16 oz. kidney, pinto or black beans
1-1/4 cup taco sauce
1-1/2 cups (6oz) shredded cheese
1/2 cup rice

Cut tops from peppers. Cook peppers until slightly tender in boiling water, about 5 minutes; drain.

Mix beans, tomatoes, 3/4 cup taco sauce, rice, 1 cup cheese, onions & coriander; mix well. Spoon into peppers. Place in shallow dish.

Bake at 350 for 30 minutes. Sprinkle remaining 1/2 cup cheese on top; let stand 5 minutes. Top with remaining 1/2 cup taco sauce to serve.

Susan Beckman

BAKED ONIONS

4 small red or yellow onions
1/2 cup olive oil
1/4 cup soy sauce
1/4 cup balsamic vinegar
1/4 cup Worcestershire
Pepper

Cut off tops & bottoms of onions, remove skins. Place onions & ingredients in plastic food storage bag & marinate at room temp. for 1 hour.

Remove onions from bag, saving 1/4 cup of marinade. Arrange onions in baker. Pour reserved marinade over onions & cover with lid.

Place in cold oven. Bake at 375 for 1 hour, basting occasionally.

BAKED CAULIFLOWER

1 large cauliflower (or frozen)
1/2 cup mayo
1/2 teaspoon salt
1/2 teaspoon curry
10 oz. cream of celery soup
1/4 cup bread crumbs
4 oz. shredded cheese
2 Tablespoons melted butter

Break cauliflower in small pieces & cook. In 2-quart casserole, mix undiluted soup, cheese, mayo & curry; add cauliflower. Toss bread crumbs with melted butter & sprinkle on top.

Bake at 350° for 45 minutes.

Can also be frozen before baking.

This was another one of my mom's holiday dishes. My girls still request it.

CREAMED CABBAGE

1 bacon strip, diced
1 teaspoon cider vinegar
1-1/4 teaspoon sugar
2 cup shredded cabbage
1/4 cup sour cream
2 teaspoon chopped onion
1 teaspoon water
1/4 teaspoon salt
Dash pepper
1 small apple, peeled & chopped

In skillet, cook bacon until crisp. Remove to paper towel. In drippings, sauté onion until tender. Add vinegar, water, sugar, salt & pepper; cook until bubbly.

Stir in cabbage & apple; toss to coat. Cover & cook 5-6 minutes or until cabbage is tender.

Stir in sour cream; heat through (do not boil). Sprinkle with bacon.

1 serving

SWEET-SOUR RED CABBAGE

1 med. red cabbage, 2 #
2 teaspoon shortening
1-3/4 cup water
1 teaspoon sugar
salt & pepper
1 sm. onion, diced
1 apple, quartered
1/2 cup mild vinegar
4 whole cloves
2 teaspoon flour

Grate or slice cabbage in small pieces. Brown onion in oil. Add rest, except flour.

Cover & cook until tender, 30-35 minutes Thicken with flour.

Susan Beckman

MISCELLANEOUS

Susan Beckman

FREEZER PICKLES

7 cup thin-sliced cucumbers
1 cup green pepper, chopped
1 cup onion, chopped

MIXTURE:
1 cup vinegar
2 cup sugar
1 teaspoon salt
1 teaspoon celery seed

Pour mixture over veggies.

Put in fridge for four days. Then freeze.

My mother-in-law and her mother made these all the time. I still can't seem to get it to taste like theirs!

Susan Beckman

YORKSHIRE PUDDING

3 eggs
1/2 cup flour
1/2 cup milk
1 teaspoon salt
Pepper
3 teaspoon melted butter or beef drippings

Preheat oven to 425. Butter molds of baking pan. Beat eggs vigorously until light yellow (about 30 seconds) Add flour & beat well. Beat in milk, salt & pepper, & butter or drippings.

Spoon into molds about 1/4" deep (half full). Place in hot oven & bake for 10 minutes Lower heat to 300 & bake another 10-12 minutes until well puffed & golden brown.

Serve hot with roast meat.

This is from a friend, Mary Hubbs, who was from England and taught me that Yorkshire pudding is not pudding-pudding - it's like a tall collapsed roll that you put gravy in. Once we discovered this news, this recipe is a "keeper."

BACON-FLAVORED DOG TREATS

5 cups whole wheat flour
1 cup milk
2 eggs
10 tablespoons bacon fat or oil
1 pinch onion or garlic powder
1/2 cup cold water
1 teaspoon salt
1 tablespoon oil to grease pan

Mix all ingredients well. Pinch off pieces of dough and roll into balls.

Bake at 350 ° for 35-40 minutes.

The dog biscuits from the stores usually didn't settle well with our dogs, so I learned to make my own dog treats.

OATMEAL WHEAT DOG BISCUIT TREATS

1 cup uncooked oatmeal
3/4 cups powdered milk
1/3 cup butter
3/4 cups cornmeal
1 teaspoon bouillon (any flavor)
1 egg
1-1/2 cups hot water
3 cups whole wheat or white flour

In large bowl, pour hot water over oatmeal, butter & bouillon; let stand 5 minutes. Stir in powdered milk, cornmeal & egg. Add flour, 1/2 cup at a time, mixing well after each addition. Knead 3-4 minutes, adding more flour if necessary to make a very stiff dough.
Pat or roll dough to 1/2" thickness or less. Cut into shapes & place on a greased baking sheet. Bake for 50 minutes at 325. Allow to cool & dry out until hard.

I save bacon drippings or other drippings and add to hot water to make 1-1/2 cups.

VEGIE THINS DOG BISCUIT TREATS

1-1/2 cups flour
1 vegetable cube or packet
1/4 cup oil
1/4 cup carrots, shredded or ground
1/4 cup powdered milk
1/4 cup boiling water
1 teaspoon. Brown sugar
1/2 egg or egg substitute

Dissolve veggie cube in boiling water. Mix dry ingredients; mix wet ingredients separately, except egg. Pour wet ingredients into dry; mix lightly. Add a well in the center and add the egg. Mix.

Place dough on lightly floured surface, sprinkle a little flour on top. Roll out to not more than 1/8". Don't use too much flour or they will puff up. Cut into shapes.

Place on ungreased cookie sheet. Bake 15 minutes, turn over & bake another 10 minutes

WESTERN RANCH DOG BISCUIT TREATS

1 package dry yeast
2 cups warm beef broth
1/2 cup honey
1/4 cup bacon grease
   or butter
2-1/2 cups flour
   (white, oat or rye)
1 cup wheat germ
3/4 cup wheat bran
3/4 cup grated cheese
Topping: 1 cup beef broth
3 teaspoon oil

1/4 cup warm water
1/4 cup milk
1 egg
1 teaspoon salt
1 cup cornmeal
1/2 tsp. garlic powder
2 cups cracked wheat
3/4 cup oatmeal
3 cups whole wheat flour

3 teaspoons oil

In small bowl, dissolve yeast in warm water. In large bowl, mix beef broth, milk, honey, egg, bacon grease or butter & salt. Add yeast/water mixture & mix well. Stir in flour, cornmeal, wheat germ, cracked wheat, wheat bran, oatmeal & cheese. Add whole wheat flour, 1/2 cup at a time, mixing well after each addition. Knead in the final amounts of flour by hand to make stiff dough. Continue to knead for 4-5 minutes. Pat or roll to 1/2" thickness. Cut into shapes & place on greased baking sheet. Cover lightly & let set (rise) for 30 minutes Bake 45 minutes at 350 or until lightly browned on bottom.

Prepare topping during last few minutes. Turn off oven. Remove biscuits from oven. Immediately dip biscuits in topping. Return them to oven & leave in oven for several hours or overnight.

OATMEAL CHEESE DOG BISCUIT TREATS

1 cup uncooked oatmeal
4 oz. (1 cup) grated cheese
1 cup wheat germ
1/2 cup powdered milk
1 cup cornmeal
1-1/2 cups hot water or meat juices
1 egg
1/4 cup butter
1/4 teaspoon salt
3 cups whole wheat flour

In large bowl, pour hot water over oatmeal & butter; let stand 5 minutes Stir in powdered milk, cheese, salt & egg. Add cornmeal & wheat germ. Mix well. Add flour, 1/3 cup at a time, mixing well after each addition. Knead 3-4 minutes, adding more flour if necessary to make stiff dough. Pat or roll dough to 1/2".

Cut into shapes & place on greased baking sheet. Bake 1 hour at 300. Turn off heat & leave in over for 1-1/2 hours or longer.

PARMESAN SNAPS DOG TREATS

1 cup uncooked oatmeal
1 cup boiling water
2 teaspoon parsley
1/2 cup milk
1 egg
1/3 cup butter
3/4 cup cornmeal
2 teaspoon bouillon (any flavor)
1 cup shredded parmesan cheese
2-3 cups whole wheat flour

Mix oatmeal, butter & water; let stand 10 minutes Stir in cornmeal, parsley, bouillon, milk, cheese & egg; mix well. Add flour 1 cup at a time, to make stiff dough. Knead in remaining flour until dough is smooth & no longer sticky, 3-4 minutes Roll or pat out dough to 1/2", cut into shapes. Place 1" apart on greased cookie sheet.

Bake 35-45 minutes at 325 or until golden brown.

GARLIC DOG BISCUIT TREATS

2-1/2 cups whole wheat flour
1/2 teaspoon salt
1 teaspoon brown sugar
1 egg
1/2 cup powdered milk
1/2 teaspoon garlic powder
6 teaspoon meat drippings
1/2 cup ice water

Mix flour, milk, salt, garlic & sugar. Cut in meat drippings until resembles cornmeal. Mix in egg. Add enough water to forms a ball.

Pat out dough onto cookie sheet to 1/2" thick. Cut with cookie cutter or knife & remove scraps. Scraps can be formed again & baked.

Bake 25-30 minutes at 350.

PEANUT BUTTER DOG BISCUIT TREATS

1-1/2 cups water
2 eggs
2 teaspoon vanilla
1-1/4 cups white flour
1/2 cup oatmeal
1/2 cup oil
3 teaspoon peanut butter
1-1/2 cups whole wheat flour
1/2 cup cornmeal

Mix water, oil, eggs, peanut butter & vanilla with wire whisk. Add flours, cornmeal & oats. Mix with a mixer.

Take a third of dough and place on floured surface. Flour top of dough. Gently knead, adding more flour as necessary to form a pliable dough (this will require a substantial amount of flour). Roll out to 1/2" to 3/4" thickness & cut into shapes. Place on ungreased baking sheet.

Bake 20-25 minutes at 400. Leave in oven 20 minutes after turning oven off to crisp.

SUPER SIMPLE CHUNKY PEANUT DOG TREATS

2 cups whole wheat flour
1 cup chunky peanut butter
1 teaspoon baking powder
1 cup milk

Mix flour & baking powder. Use another bowl & mix peanut butter & milk. Add the milk/peanut butter mixture to the dry ingredients & mix well.

On floured surface, turn out & knead. Roll out to 1/4" thickness. Cut into shapes.

Place on greased baking sheets & bake 20 minutes at 375, or until lightly browned.

Susan Beckman

MICROWAVE DOG BISCUIT TREATS

1 cup whole wheat flour
1/4 cup cornmeal
1 teaspoon bouillon granules
1/2 cup quick-cooking oatmeal
1 egg
3/4 cup powdered milk
1/3 cup shortening
1/2 cup plain flour
1 teaspoon sugar
1/2 cup hot water

Mix flour, cornmeal, milk, oatmeal & sugar. Cut in shortening. Add egg, bouillon & hot water. Knead 5 minutes.

Roll 1/2" thick & cut into shapes. Microwave at 50% powder for 5-10 minutes, rotating plate.

MULTI-GRAIN DOG BISCUIT TREATS

3-1/2 cups white flour
1 cup rye flour
2 cups cracked wheat (bulgur)
4 teaspoon salt
1 package dry yeast
2 cups whole wheat flour
1 cup cornmeal
1/2 cup powdered milk
2 cups chicken stock
1 egg
1 teaspoon milk

Mix in big bowl, the flours, cornmeal, milk powder & salt. In separate bowl, dissolve yeast in 1/4 cup lukewarm water; let sit for a few minutes until bubbly. Add chicken stock to the yeast mixture; mix well. Add the liquid to the dry ingredients. Knead about 3 minutes Dough should be stiff. Flour board with cornmeal & roll out to 1/4" thick. Cut into shapes & place on ungreased cookie sheets. Mix the egg & milk & use to brush tops of biscuits (for shine), then bake for 45 minutes at 300.

Turn off heat & leave in oven overnight. This makes them bone-hard.

BABY BEEF DOG TREATS

2-3/4 cups whole wheat flour
1 teaspoon salt
1 egg
8-10 teaspoon water
1/2 cup powdered milk
1/4 teaspoon garlic powder
6 teaspoon oil
2 small jars strained baby food
(beef, chicken, lamb or liver)

Mix all ingredients together in large bowl & knead for 3 minutes. Roll out to 1/2" thick. Cut into shapes & place on ungreased baking sheet.

Bake for 20-25 minutes at 350.

Farmhouse Cookbook

Susan Beckman

DIY

Susan Beckman

ANTIPASTO SALAD DRESSING

9 oz. oil (10% olive oil)
6 oz. red vinegar
1 oz. lemon juice
1 teaspoon oregano
1 teaspoon garlic powder
1/2 teaspoon pepper
1/2 teaspoon salt
1/2 teaspoon onion powder

Mix all in a 16-ounce jar or bottle and shake before using.

HIDDEN VALLEY RANCH DRESSING MIX

15 saltine crackers
2 cups dry parsley
1 tablespoon minced onion
2 tablespoons dill weed
1/4 teaspoon onion salt
1/4 teaspoon garlic salt
1/4 teaspoon onion powder
1/4 teaspoon garlic powder

Dump all ingredients in food processor & blend until completely powdered.

TO USE:

Mix 1 tablespoon dry mix with 1 cup mayo & 1 cup buttermilk.

I don't like using things with MSG, so I searched for a recipe for this dressing mix and voila!

SHAKE & BAKE MIX

1 cup bread crumbs
1/2 teaspoon salt
1/2 cup flour
1/2 teaspoon pepper
2 teaspoons onion powder
2 teaspoons dried celery or dried onion
1 teaspoon garlic powder
2 teaspoons poultry season
1/2 teaspoon cayenne
1 teaspoon paprika

Mix & store for 6 to 12 months.

Dip any kind of meat in 1/2 cup milk & 1 egg. Then coat with Shake & Bake mix. Lay on foil-lined baking sheet

Bake at 375° for 1 hour.

There is no difference between this recipe and the store bought - and I helped!

Susan Beckman

TACO SEASONING MIX

1 cup dried onion
1/3 cup dry beef bouillon
4 teaspoon crushed red pepper
1 tablespoon oregano
1/3 cup chili powder
2 tablespoon ground cumin

Mix & store for 4 months.

One tablespoon is equal to one packet of taco seasoning mix.

Do you ever not have that little packet of taco seasoning mix when you need it? Here's how to make your own.

FROSTY PAWS

32 oz. yogurt
2 teaspoon honey
2 heaping teaspoon peanut butter (or more)
Ripe banana or jar of banana baby food

Mix & freeze in small containers.

My dogs love these!

BAKING PAN GREASE

1 cup margarine
1 cup flour
1 cup shortening

Mix in Kitchen Aid mixer until smooth.

Store at room temp. up to 1 week; in fridge for 2 months; in freezer for 1 year.

This works great for cake pans. You don't have the mess of shaking flour around a pan coated with grease. Just wipe this in the pan and the cake doesn't stick.

BISQUICK

4 cup flour
1-1/2 teaspoon salt
1/2 cup shortening
2 teaspoon baking powder
2 teaspoon sugar

In stand mixer, combine flour, baking powder, sugar & salt until well mixed.

While mixer is going, slowly cut in shortening.

Mix for 1 full minute.

Store in airtight container or freeze for 3-4 weeks.

This turns out exactly the same as store bought.

Susan Beckman

SOURDOUGH STARTER

3/4 cup (4 oz.)+ 2
teaspoon flour w/4 oz.
water

DAY 1: Stir vigorously into a sticky, thick batter. Cover container with plastic wrap & leave on counter.

DAY 2: Stir occasionally. Should start bubbling.

DAY 3: Should be bubbly. Add 4 oz. flour & 4 oz. water (smooth).

DAY 4: Should be double. Feed same as Day 3.

DAY 5: Test by dropping a teaspoon of starter in glass of water. If it floats, it's ready; if not, give another day & more feeding.

DAY 6: Maintaining: Discard half & keep feeding same amount flour & water daily. If not using often, cover & place in fridge. Feed at least once a week.

MAYONNAISE

2 eggs
1 teaspoon lemon juice
1 teaspoon dry mustard
1 teaspoon salt
2 cup oil

Add all to blender, except only 1/4 cup oil. Blend on high speed immediately.

Add remaining oil in slow, steady stream, until blended.

Susan Beckman

CHOCOLATE PUDDING MIX

2-1/2 cup dry milk
5 cup sugar
3 cup cornstarch
1 teaspoon salt
2-1/2 cup cocoa

Mix & store. Stir before using.

2/3 cup mix with 2 cup milk – cook over low heat to boil; stir 1 minutes

Remove & chill.

VANILLA PUDDING MIX

3 cup dry milk
3 cup sugar
1 teaspoon salt
3 cup cornstarch
1 vanilla bean

Mix all & cut bean in large pieces. Stir before using.

1/2 cup mix with 2 cup milk. Cook over low heat to boil. Stir 1 minute.

Remove & chill.

GOULASH (DEHYDRATE)

1 teaspoon olive oil
1 cup onion, chopped
1 teaspoon salt
½ teaspoon pepper
7 oz. macaroni
1-1/2 pounds ground turkey
1 teaspoon garlic
½ teaspoon oregano
28 oz. can tomatoes

Saute oil, turkey & onion until onions are cook. Stir often to break mixture into small pieces. Add seasonings & tomatoes. Reduce heat to medium low and cook until most of liquid has evaporated. Remove from heat. Allow to cool.

Lightly oil 2 fruit roll sheets. Spread 2 cups evenly on each sheet. Dry at 145 for 6 hours or until dry. Store in air-tight container.

TO REHYDRATE: Put contents in pan, add 2 cups boiling water, cover, stir and allow to rehydrate for 30 minutes. Remove cover & cook on high heat. Boil 2 cups water & add macaroni. Cover & remove from heat for 10 minutes. Add to pan. Stir & serve. Serves 4-6.

CHEX MIX

3 cups Corn Chex cereal
3 cups Rice Chex cereal
3 cups Wheat Chex cereal
1 cup mixed nuts
1 cup bite-size pretzels
1 cup garlic-flavor bite-size bagel chips

6 tablespoons butter
2 tablespoons Worcestershire
1-1/2 teaspoon seasoned salt
3/4 teaspoon garlic powder
1/2 teaspoon onion powder

In large microwavable bowl, mix cereals, nuts, pretzels & bagel chips; set aside. In small bowl, microwave butter uncovered on high about 40 seconds or until melted. Stir in seasonings. Pour over cereal mixture; stir until evenly coated. Microwave uncovered on high 5-6 minutes, thoroughly stirring every 2 minutes. Spread on paper towels to cool. Store in airtight container.

Oven Directions:

Heat oven to 250. Bake 1 hour, stirring every 15 minutes. Spread on paper towels to cool, about 15 minutes. Store in airtight container.

Can add other spices to your taste - like cayenne pepper!

Susan Beckman

TIPS

Susan Beckman

10 Foods You Should Be Eating Every Day

1. **Flaxseeds**
   An easy way to add a big dose of fiber into your diet. Can be sprinkled over salads, fish or any type of meal or snack. A single tablespoon of ground flaxseed provides an easy 2.3 grams of fiber. But they must be ground. I've heard there is no advantage if you eat them whole.

2. **Beans**
   The soluble fiber found in beans soaks up cholesterol, allowing your body to dispose of it before it sticks to your artery walls. Also proven to be one of the best sources of antioxidants.

3. **Blueberries**
   A better source of antioxidants than 40 other common fruits. You'll get the most bang for your buck with this delicious fruit.

4. **Yogurt**
   Single serving gives a significant amount of calcium for the day. Most yogurts are a great source of probiotics, which protect your stomach against harmful bacterias that could lead to infection or illness.

5. **Oats**
   Proven to lower cholesterol and blood pressure. 1-1/2 cups of cooked oatmeal provides enough beta-glucan to lower blood cholesterol by about 5 percent and heart attack risk by about 10 percent.

6. **Broccoli**

The sulfur compounds found in broccoli signal our genes to increase production of enzymes and detoxify potentially cancer-causing compounds.

7. **Eggs**
   A great source of high quality protein. Also known to fill you up, preventing you from snacking on unhealthy mini-meals throughout the day. Eggs also help keep your eye health in check.

8. **Spinach**
   A great source of vitamins A, C and K, as well as some fiber, iron, calcium, potassium, magnesium and vitamin E.

9. **Mixed Nuts**
   Great source of heart-healthy unsaturated fats. A recent study reveals that adults who consumed nuts on a regular basis were likely to live 2 years long than their non-nut-eating counterparts. Walnuts and almonds are best options

10. **Oranges**
    Eating one large, fresh orange will give you 100 percent of your daily recommended vitamin C. Likewise, 1 cup of 100 percent pure orange juice will do the same. It is also high in fiber and folate.

SUGGESTIONS FOR SEASONING

Add the herb or spice to the meat or cooking water.

<u>Chicken</u>
Thyme
Parsley
Rosemary
Sage

<u>Lamb</u>
Curry powder
Rosemary
Garlic
Saffron
Mint

<u>Veal</u>
Thyme
Marjoram

<u>Pork</u>
Sage
Onion
Rosemary
Oregano

<u>Beef</u>
Bay leaf
Pepper
Onion
Green pepper
Marjoram
Ginger
Cumin

<u>Seafood</u>
Bay leaf
Parsley
Basil
Onion
Lemon
Mace
Savory

<u>Eggs</u>
Onion
Green pepper
Oregano
Basil
Parsley
Celery seed
Black or red pepper

VEGETABLES

<u>Asparagus</u>
Onion
Lemon

<u>Green Beans</u>
Onion

<u>Squash</u>
Pepper
Garlic
Onion
Cinnamon

Carrots
Cinnamon
Nutmeg
Cloves
Allspice
Mint
Chives

Peas
Nutmeg
Mint
Onion
Celery seed
Savory

Beets
Cloves
Vinegar

Potatoes
Onion
Parsley
Garlic

Lima Beans
Pepper
Onion

Corn
Green pepper
Onion
Pepper

Basil
Onion
Bay leaf

FRUITS

Apples
Cinnamon
Nutmeg
Cloves

Bananas
Lemon

Peaches
Cinnamon
Nutmeg
Cloves

Pears
Mint

Pineapple
Mint

Tomato

BREADS

Add to dough or to butter for them.

Garlic
Lemon
Orange
Cinnamon
Nutmeg
onion

SUBSTITUTIONS FOR INGREDIENTS

1 tablespoon cornstarch (for thickening)
> 2 tablespoons flour

1 cup sifted cake flour
> 1 cup minus 2 tablespoons sifted all-purpose flour

1 cup sour milk
> 1 cup milk into which 1 tablespoon vinegar or lemon juice has been stirred

1 square chocolate (1 ounce)
> 3 or 4 tablespoons cocoa plus 1/2 tablespoon fat

1 cup sifted all-purpose flour
> 1 cup plus 2 tablespoons sifted cake flour

1 cup milk
> 1 cup sour milk or buttermilk plus 1/2 teaspoon baking soda

1 cup cream, sour, thin
> 3 tablespoons butter and 3/4 cup milk in sour milk recipe

1 whole egg
> 2 egg yolks

1 cup molasses
> 1 cup honey

1 package active dry yeast
    1 cake compressed yeast

1 tablespoon instant minced onion, dehydrated
    1 small fresh onion

1 tablespoon prepared mustard
    1 teaspoon dry mustard

1 tablespoon fresh herbs
    1 teaspoon dried

1 cup honey
    1-1-1/4 cups sugar + 1/4 cup liquid

1 cup butter
    7/8 to 1 cup lard or hydrogenated fat + 1/2 teaspoon salt

1 cup fresh whole milk
    1 cup reconstituted dry milk + 2 teaspoons butter

1 cup whole milk
    1/2 cup evaporated milk + 1/2 cup water

HOW MUCH TO BUY

MEAT		WEIGHT	# of SERVINGS
BEEF	Round steak	1 pound	3 to 4
	Porterhouse steak	1 pound	2
	Sirloin steak	2 pounds	4
	Chuck Roast	2 pounds	4 to 6
	Rib Roast (bone in)	4 pounds	8
	Short Ribs	1 pound	1 to 2
	Stew Meat	1 pound	4 to 5
	Hamburger	1 pound	4
POULTRY	Chicken Fryer	2-3 pounds	3 to 5
	Chicken Broiler	1-2 pounds	2 to 3
	Chicken Roaster	2-7 pounds	4 to 10
	Turkey	8 pounds	16
FISH	Steaks	1 pound	3
	Fillets	1 pound	4
	Whole Fish	1 pound	1
SHELLFISH	Lobster (tails)	1 pound	2
	Lobster (cooked meat)	1 pound	2
	Clams (shucked)	1 pint	3
	Shrimp (cooked)	1 pound	5 to 6
	Oysters (shucked)	1 pint	3
	Oysters (cooked)	1 pound	6
	Scallops	1 pound	6

EQUIVALENTS

Apples	1 medium	1 cup sliced
Bread Crumbs	3-4 slices bread	1 cup dry crumbs
	1 slice bread	3/4 cup soft crumbs
Cabbage	1 pound	4 cups shredded
Cheese	1/4 pound	1 cup shredded
Cherries	1 quart	2 cups pitted
Crackers,		
Graham	15	1 cup fine crumbs
Soda	16	1 cup coarse crumbs
	22	a cup fine crumbs
Cranberries sauce	1 pound	3 to 3-1/2 cups
Cream,		
Whipping	1 cup	2 cups whipped
Raisins	1 pound	3 cups, seedless
		2-1/2 cups, seeded
Dates	1 pound	2-1/2 cups, chopped
Dry Beans	1 cup	2-1/2 cups cooked
Eggs	5 medium	1 cup
	8 medium egg whites	1 cup
	12-13 medium egg yolks	1 cup

Flour	1 pound sifted	4 cups
Lemon	1	2-3 tablespoons juice
Pasta	1/2 pound	4 cups cooked
Nuts		
Peanuts	5 ounces	1 cup
Pecans, chop	4-1/2 ounces	1 cup
halves	3-3/4 ounces	1 cup
Walnuts, chop	4-1/2 ounces	1 cup
halves	3-1/2 ounces	1 cup
Onion	1 medium	1/2 cup chopped
Orange	1	1/3 to 1/2 cup juice
Rice	1 cup	3-1/2 cups cooked
Precooked	1 cup	2 cups cooked
Sugar		
Brown packed	1 pound	2-1/3 cups firm
Powdered	1 pound	3-1/2 cups sifted
White	1 pound	2-1/4 cups

WEIGHTS & MEASURES

Pinch	1/8 teaspoon or less
1 tablespoon	3 teaspoons
4 tablespoons	1/4 cup
8 tablespoons	1/2 cup
12 tablespoons	3/4 cup
1 cup liquid	1/2 pint
2 cups liquid	1 pint
4 cups liquid	1 quart
2 pints liquid	1 quart
4 quarts	1 gallon
8 quarts	1 peck (apples, pears, etc.)
16 ounces	1 pound

Susan Beckman

ABOUT THE AUTHOR

Susan Beckman is a Christian, a sister, a wife, a mother, a grandmother, a great-grandmother, a friend, and a COOK.

Susan has published *The Special Chosen One, 10 Critical Guidelines to Begin Searching for Your Birth Family,* and *The Unforgettable Angel.* She has published short stories in newsletters, booklets, newspapers, and magazines, such as *Breakthrough Intercessor, Victory Herald, Living Stones News, Christian Citizen USA,* and *City Light News.*

Susan was born and raised in Michigan and met her husband in high school in Ohio, where they were married in 1973. They have lived in Marquette, Michigan; Van Wert, Ohio; Toledo, Ohio; and in Florida since 1982.

They have two daughters, four grandchildren, and one great-grandson. She is blessed to have them living nearby, giving her the pleasure to be actively involved and participate in their lives, both socially and spiritually, and the opportunity to COOK for them.

Susan lives in the country and enjoys decorating their home in old-fashioned farmhouse style. In addition to reading and writing, she enjoys Bible studies, quilting, candlemaking, herbology, COOKING, canning, genealogy, crocheting, knitting, spinning, and gardening.

She would love to hear from you!

Email: sbeckmanauthor@aol.com
Web site: www.susanbeckman.com
FB: www.facebook.com/SusanBeckmanAuthor
Twitter: @beckmansb

Proverbs 31

Susan Beckman

NOTES

Susan Beckman

Susan Beckman

INDEX

APPETIZERS & SNACKS

Shrimp Cheese Balls 7
Crab Spread 8
Olive-Cheese Balls 9
Surprise Meatballs 10
Seasoned Crackers 11
Fruit & Nut Mix 12
Knox Blocks 13
Bang Bang Shrimp 14
Fried Dill Pickles 15
Sugared Pecans 16
Cheese Ball 17
Goat Cheese stuffed Basil Leaves 18
Sausage Cups 19
Granola 20
Cowboy Candy 21

BEANS

Beans, Beans, Beans 27
Easy Baked Beans 28
Old-Fashioned Baked Beans 29
Bean Salad 30
Marinated Green Beans with Tomatoes,
   Olives & Feta 31

BEEF

Porcupine Meatballs 35
Hungarian Pig in the Blanket 36

BEEF
(Continued)

Mississippi Redneck Roast 37
Beef Tenderloin 38
Beef Bourg...39
....
Brisket with Cranberry Gravy........................40
Sauerbraten 41
Swiss Steak 42
Texas Hash...43
Mary Ann's Swedish Meatballs.....................44
Beef Jerky 45

BREADS & MUFFINS

Beer Bread 51
Bread Sticks 52
Dumplings..53
Cheddar Biscuits 54
Amish Cinnamon Bread.................................55
Sourdough Banana Bread 56
Ready Morning Muffins 57
English Tea Muffins 58
Monkey Bread..59
Parmesan-Parsley Biscuit Flatbread 60
Rosemary-Garlic Biscuit Flatbread................61
Swiss Cheese Bread 62
Cranberry Orange Bread 63
No-Excuse Bread 64
Dark Date Nut Bread 65
No-Knead Whole Wheat Fridge Rolls...........66
Apple Cider Biscuits 67
Baking Powder Biscuits.................................68

BREADS & MUFFINS
(Continued)

Good-Morning Muffins 69
Rye Bread..70

BEVERAGES

Southern Sweet Tea 75
Russian Tea..76
Kahlua..77
Orange Brutus 78
Hot Cocoa Mix..79
Red Zinger Tea 80
Brandy Slush...81

CAKES & CUPCAKES

Black-Bottom Cupcakes 85
Red Velvet Cake 86
Nancy's Loaf Cake 87
Butter Brickle Dessert...................................88
Pumpkin Pie Cake...89
Fudge Brownie Ring Cake............................90
Pineapple Upside-Down Cake 91
Texas Chocolate Sheet Cake.........................92
Turtle Cake..93
Pistachio Cake...94
Cocoa-Almond Cake.....................................95
Carrot Cake 96
Chocolate Velvet Cheesecake.......................97
Coca-Cola Cake 98

CAKES & CUPCAKES
(Continued)

Hot Fudge Pudding Cake 99
Apple Cake 100

CANDY

Salted Caramel Pretzel Bark 105
Daddy's Fudge 106
Elaine's Fudge 107
Peppermint Bark 108
Salty Chocolate-Pecan Candy 109
Tootsie Rolls 110
Mixed Nut Bars 111
Cracker Jacks 112
Buckeyes 113
Caramels 114
No-Cook Divinity 115
Caramel Corn 116
Taffy 117
Rum Balls 118

CASSEROLES

Turkey Casserole 123
Sausage & Cheese Grits 124
Chicken Rice Casserole 125
Tuna-Broccoli Casserole 126
Reuben Casserole 127
Johnny Marzetti Casserole 128
Amish After Church 5-in-1 Casserole 129
Vegan Solyanka 130

CASSEROLES
(Continued)

9-Layer Casserole 131
Chicken & Broccoli Rice Casserole 132
Annetta Good's Yum-A-Setti 133
Chicken & Wild Rice Casserole 134
Macaroni-Bacon Casserole 135
California Casserole 136
Judy's Baked Spaghetti 137
Pasta & Spinach Casserole 138

CHICKEN

Chicken Wonder 143
Poppy Seed Chicken 144
Wonderful Moist Chicken 145
Moo Goo Gai Pan 146
Chicken & Dumplings 147
Chicken Breasts Saute Sec 148
Herbed Chicken & Orzo 149
Chicken & Broccoli Alfredo 150
Chicken Fried Steak 151
Chicken Cordon Bleu 152
Pecan Chicken Tenders Salad 153
St. Stephen's Chicken Paprikash 154
Deviled Chicken 155
Greek Chicken 156
Cashew Chicken 157
Apricot Chicken 158
Poppy Seed Chicken 159
Marrakesh Chicken 160
Orange-Glazed Chicken 161

CHICKEN
(Continued)

Spanish Chicken with Rice & Beans 162
Chicken Breasts Florentine 163
Famous Restaurant Chicken & Dumplings....164
Chicken Martha...165

COOKIES

Sugar Bar Cookies 169
Sugar Bar Cookie Frosting..............................170
Sweet & Saltines 171
Holly Cookies 172
Lemon Pie Cookies 173
One-Bowl Brownies..174
Graham Cracker Cookies................................175
Amish Peanut Butter Cookies 176
Forgotten Cookies...177
Amish Monster Cookies 178
Clum Christmas Cookies 179
Oatmeal Cinnamon Chip Cookies 180
Amish Sugar Cookies 181
Kolacky 182
Carmelitas 183
Magic Cookie Bars 184
Congo Squares 185
Choosy Cheese Bars 186
Sour Cream Pumpkin Bars..............................187
Browned Butter Frosting.................................188
Oaty Rhubarb Streusel Bars............................189
Ginger Icing 190
Seeded Cookies...191

COOKIES
(Continued)

Snickerdoodles 192
La Leche League Oatmeal Cookies 193
Brownie Chip Cookies 194
Molasses Oatmeal Cookies 195
Unbaked Oatmeal Balls 196
Potato Chip Cookies 197
Pumpkin Cookies 198
Gauflettes 199
Best Cookies You Ever Ate 200
Mamau's Cream Wafer Cookies 201
Macaroons 202
Angel Wings 203

DESSERTS

Strawberry Pretzel Dessert 209
Amish Bread Pudding 210
Peach Cobbler 211
Crisp Cherry Surprise 212
Rice Krispie Treats 213
Berries with Mascarpone & Meringue 214
Blueberry Delight 215
Pineapple Delight 216
Pineapple Crisp 217
Apple Brown Betty 218
Cinnamon Crisp 219
Fruit Crisp 220
Rhubarb-Cherry Crunch 221
Minty Mallows 222
Fruit Cobbler 223

DESSERTS
(Continued)

Southern Nut Dessert 224
Tina's Chocolate Graham Dessert 225
Impossible Brownie Pie 226
Indoor S'Mores 227
Oreo Pie Pudding 228
Strawberry Parfait 229
Lemon Squares..230

DIPS

Jalapeno Popper Dip 235
Spinach Artichoke Dip....................................236
Mary Jo's Bean Dip 237
Slow Ball Dip..238
Hot Tamale Dip...239
Vegie Dip 240
Crab Dip..241
Easy Greek Dip 242

EGGS

Bacon & Cheese Oven Omelet 247
Hard-Boiled Eggs..248
Egg Rolls...249
Eggs Benedict 250
Hollandaise Sauce 251
Eggs with Celery Sauce 252
Mushroom Frittata 253

FROSTINGS

Red Velvet Cake Frosting 259
Clum Christmas Cookie Frosting 260
Mamau's Frosting 261

HAM

Ham Bake 265
Colcannon 266
Golden Glaze Ham 267
Ham Loaf 268
Crock Pot Ham & Scalloped Potatoes 269
Glazed Ham Loaf 270

JELLIES & JAMS

Strawberry Jam 275
Plum Jam 276
Lemon-Honey Jelly 277

MAIN COURSES

GB Slop 283
Hungarian Goulash 284
Stroganoff 285
Campfire Kitchen 286
Boiled Dinner 287
Steak Supper in Foil 288
Shipwreck 289
California Tacos 290
Shepherd's Pie 291
Pasty 292

MAIN COURSES
(Continued)

Impossible Lasagne Pie 294
Impossible Taco Pie 295
Impossible Quesadilla Pie 296
Skillet-Style Lasagna 297
Skillet Macaroni Dinner 298
Jiffy Goulash 299
Frittata 300
Paprikash Burgonya 301
Tomato Tart 302
Spaghetti Pie 303
Taco Pie 304
Summer Pizza 305
Sausage & Spinach Pie 306

PASTA

Susan's Mediterranean Pasta 311
Lemon-Garlic Spaghetti 312
Mamau's Noodles 313
Macaroni with Zucchini & 3 Cheeses 314
Double-Cheese Macaroni & Cheese 315
Stuffed Shells 316
Manicotti 317
Lasagne 318
Vegie Lo Mein 319
Tagliatelle with Gorgonzola & Walnuts 320
Linguine & Shrimp 321

PASTRY

Pizza Dough 325
Pie Crust 326

PIES

Apple Pie with Oatmeal Topping 331
Nantucket Cranberry Pie 332
Fresh Fruit Pie 333
Apple Crumb Pie 334
Cross Creek Lime Pie 335
Banana Mallow Pie 336
Brown Sugar Chess Pie 337
Turtle Pumpkin Pie 338
Caramel Apple Pie 339
Oat Pastry 341
Pecan Pie 342
French Silk Chocolate Pie 343
Amish Sugar Cream Pie 344
Pumpkin Pie 345

PORK

Cherry Pork Chops 349
Lemon-Basil Pork Chops 350
Jambalaya 351
Saucy Pork & Noodle Bake 352
Stir-Fry Pork with Baby Corn 353
Roast Pork 354
BBQ Curried Pork Chops 355
Sweet/Sour Pork 356

PORK
(Continued)

BBQ Pork Chops 357
Judy's Pork Chops 358

POTATOES

Bake Potato Casserole.....................................363
Parslied Potatoes 364
Frozen Potato Casserole.................................365
Sweet Potato Casserole...................................366
Spuds A-la Elegant 367
Baked Potato Wedges 368
Baked Potato Slices...369
Shaker-Style Stewed Potatoes........................370
Hasselback Potatoes..371
Mashed Potato Cakes......................................372
Sliced Baked Potatoes.....................................373
Stuffed Baked Potatoes 374
Potato-Cheese Balls 375
Mashed Potatoes 376
Potato Thing..377
Re-Baked Potatoes 378
Potato Ratatouille..379

PRESERVES

Pickled Watermelon Rind...............................383
Caramel Spice Pear Butter.............................384

RICE

Spanish Rice with Beef 389
Grandma's Rice Pudding 390
Rice-A-Roni 391
Spinach-Pea Risotto 392
Slow Cooker Risotto 393
Asparagus-Leek Risotto 394
Rosy Beet Risotto 395
Cuban Fried Rice 396
Beef Burgundy with Rice 397
Fried Rice 398
Spanish Rice 399
Anju's Rice 400
Nameless Rice 401

SALADS

BLT Salad 407
Mom's Macaroni Salad 408
Broccoli Salad 409
5-Cup Salad 410
Layered Lettuce Salad 411
Oriental Chicken Salad 412
Georgia Cracker Salad 413
Kidney Bean Salad 414
Dutch Lettuce 415
Mixed Vegie Salad 416
Hardtack Salad 417
Golden Potato Salad 418
Spinach Salad 419
Coca-Cola Salad 420
Juliet's Ribbon Salad 421

SALADS
(Continued)

Lime Jell-O Salad 422
Fruited Gingerale Salad 423
Orange Tapioca Jell-O 424
Garden Greek Pasta Salad.................................... 425
Midsummer Macaroni Salad................................ 426
Hidden Valley Ranch Tortellini Salad.......... 427
Pasta & Kidney Beans 428
Black Bean Orzo Salad 429
Tortellini Woodsmen Style................................. 430
Mediterranean Orzo Salad 431
Italian Garden Salad... 432
Jell-O in a Can 433
Mexicorn-Bean Salad.. 434
Taffy Apple Salad 435
Ice Cream Salad 436
Greek Salad... 437
Cranberry Frost Salad 438
Ambrosia Freeze Salad 439
Cottage Cheese & Pineapple Salad................. 440
Waldorf Salad 441
White Bean & Tomato Salad 442
Pistachio Nut Salad 443
Crunch Pea Salad 444
Carrot-Raisin Salad 445
Sauerkraut Salad 446
Mexican Salad... 447
Hot Mexican Beef Salad 448
Broccoli Cole Slaw 449
Black Bean Orzo Salad 450
Greek Chicken Salad.. 451

SALADS
(Continued)

Salad with Oranges & Goat Cheese 452
Pork Salad with Ginger-Pineapple 453
Pizza Pizzazz Salad 454
Sunshine Salad 455
Ramen Noodle Salad 456
Rob's Cole Slaw 457

SANDWICHES

Oven Grilled Cheese 461
Best Darn Ham Sandwiches 462
Sandwich Spread 463
Ham Sandwich 464
A&W BBQ Beed Sandwiches 465
Crock Pot Sloppy Joes 466
Susan's Tofu Sandwich Spread 467
Homemade From Scratch Sloppy Joes 468
Frankenburgers 469
Baked Pizza Sandwich 470
Peppers & Almonds on Sourdough 471
Monte Cristo Sandwich 472
Panini Avocado Bacon Sandwich 473

SAUCES

Tartar Sauce 477
Pesto 478
Maple Syrup 479
Honey Butter 480
Pizza Sauce 481

SAUCES
(Continued)

Seafood Cocktail Sauce 482
Tina's Sweet/Sour Sauce 483
Gorgonzola Sauce 484
Red Eye Gravy 485
BBQ Sauce...486
Horsie Sauce 487
Tina's Taco Sauce..488
Saunder's Hot Fudge Sundae Topping 489

SOUPS

Broccoli & Cheese Soup................................493
Teresa Dallas' Vegie Soup.............................494
Free Soup 495
Susan's Soup 496
Kandy's Vegetable Soup................................497
Cream of Mushroom Soup.............................498
Baked Potato Soup...499
Creole Soup Pot 500
Autumn Soup 501
Hot & Sour Soup...502
Vichyssoise 503
Hamburger Soup 504
Bean Soup 505
Fass 506
Autumn Chowder..507
Cuban Black Bean Soup 508
Beef, Barley & Kale Soup 509
Greek Lemon Soup 510
Golden Broth...511

SOUPS
(Continued)

French Onion Soup 512
Tina's Broccoli Soup 513
Country Corn Chowder..........................514

STEWS

Emma Lou's Stew over Rice 519
Oven Stew...520
Cincinnati Chili.......................................521
French Oven Stew...................................522
Wendy's Chili..523

TOMATOES

Fried Green Tomatoes..............................527
Michelle's Tomato Pie 528
Sauteed Tomatoes 529

VEGGIES

Beets with Orange Sauce 533
Copper Pennies 534
Sunshine Carrots 535
Gold Carrot Bake 536
Fried Corn 537
Baked Stuffed Cucumbers 538
Roasted Garlic..539
Quick Corn Mazatlán................................540
Corn Fritters 541
Succotash 542

VEGGIES
(Continued)

Carrots 543
Broccoli Cheese Squares 544
Broccoli & Cheese 545
Vegetable Fritter Batter 546
Baked Zucchini 547
Baked Spinach & Cheese 548
Brussel Sprouts with Water Chestnuts 549
Peas in Orange Dill Sauce 550
Stuffed Peppers 551
Baked Onions 552
Baked Cauliflower 553
Creamed Cabbage 554
Sweet-Sour Red Cabbage 555

MISCELLANEOUS

Freezer Pickles 559
Yorkshire Pudding 560
Bacon-Flavored Dog Treats 561
Oatmeal Wheat Dog Biscuit Treats 562
Vegie Thins Dog Biscuit Treats 563
Western Ranch Dog Biscuit Treats 564
Oatmeal Cheese Dog Biscuit Treats 565
Parmesan Snaps Dog Treats 566
Garlic Dog Biscuit Treats 567
Peanut Butter Dog Biscuit Treats 568
Super Simple Peanut Butter Dog Treats 569
Microwave Dog Biscuit Treats 570
Multi-Grain Dog Biscuit Treats 571
Baby Beef Dog Treats 572

DIY

Antipasto Salad Dressing 577
Hidden Valley Ranch Dressing Mix 578
Shake & Bake Mix 579
Taco Seasoning Mix 580
Frosty Paws 581
Baking Pan Grease 582
Bisquick 583
Sourdough Starter 584
Mayonnaise 585
Chocolate Pudding Mix 586
Vanilla Pudding Mix 587
Goulash (Dehydrated) 588
Check Mix 589

TIPS

10 Foods to Eat Every Day 593
Suggestions for Seasoning 595
Substitutions for Ingredients 598
How Much to Buy 600
Equivalents 601
Weights & Measures 603

www.ingramcontent.com/pod-product-compliance
Lightning Source LLC
Chambersburg PA
CBHW020726160426
43192CB00006B/127